Scrap
FabricCrafts
Ed & Stevie Baldwin

This book was prepared especially for Better Homes and Gardens Book Clubs.

Created by The Family Workshop, Inc.

Art Director: D. Curtis Hale
Photography: Mel Root
Design for Christmas Angel: Patricia Vastine
Production: Jacqueline Nelson
Editing: Sue Puckitt and Annabelle Thompson

For HPBooks:

Publishers: Bill and Helen Fisher
Executive Editor: Carl Shipman
Editorial Director: Rick Bailey
Editor: Carlene Tejada

Published by: HPBooks
Box 5367
Tucson, AZ 85703
602-888-2150

ISBN: 0-89586-154-2
Library of Congress Catalog Card Number: 82-80109
© 1982 The Family Workshop, Inc. Printed in U.S.A.

Cover projects (clockwise from center background): Kitchen Witch, p. 58; Schoolhouse Diaper Bag, p. 16; Amy Doll p. 19; Homespun Chicken Pillow, p. 146; Handmade Christmas Ornaments, p. 76; Calico Baskets, p. 143; Padded Fabric Frame, p. 158; Tiny Tim Doll, p. 86; Baby Honeybear, p. 13; Autumn Leaves Clock, p. 64.

This book is dedicated in loving memory to
Anna Parthenia Wilhite

FOREWORD

I know you've heard that mountain climbers climb "because it's there." And this book was written for the same reason — because a mountain of remnants was there!

There is something so terribly immoral and wasteful about throwing away a perfectly good fabric scrap (no matter how small) that I simply cannot bring myself to do it. So I carefully fold it and put it away in the "scrap drawer." When my scrap drawer grew to the size that it took an entire dresser to house it, I knew something had to give. Unfortunately, fabric remnants are not like edible leftovers, which conveniently spoil so you can throw them out later without a guilty conscience.

Once you start creating with remnants, it is really rather a good and virtuous feeling since you are making something from nothing. Most of the projects in this book are now somewhere around our house, although some have been given as gifts (my mother has the "Happy Birthday Pillow" and my niece takes care of "Amy Doll").

It is our hope that this book will provide many hours of pleasure during and after you make these projects. And think of all the extra drawer space you will be getting in the bargain!

Stevie

Tips and Techniques:
Hints to help you on your way.

Enlarging a pattern

To enlarge a design draw the identical number of 1-inch squares in the same arrangement as the original grid on a larger piece of paper. Transfer the enlarged design to your fabric using carbon paper and a pencil.

Fabric painting

To begin fabric painting, you need only a starter kit of artist's acrylics containing red, blue, yellow, black and white. With these 5 colors, you can mix any other color. For example:

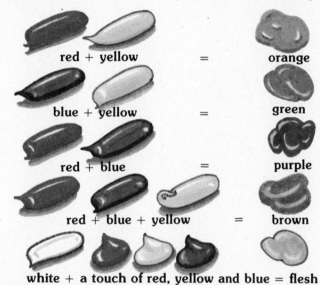

red + yellow = orange

blue + yellow = green

red + blue = purple

red + blue + yellow = brown

white + a touch of red, yellow and blue = flesh

Adding black to any color makes it darker.
Adding white to any color makes it lighter.
In general, colors specified above are mixed in equal proportions, but vary slightly with manufacturers. Mix enough of a color to complete the portion of the design you are working on, since it is very difficult to match a color later.

Acrylic paint straight from the tube is usually a good thickness for fabric painting. If the paint begins to dry while you are working with it, add a drop of water and stir thoroughly. A paint that is too watery will bleed into the fabric; paint that is too thick will not penetrate the fibers.

Begin working at the top of the design and work down. This eliminates the need to place hands and brushes on already painted work. Protect the surface below by placing a piece of aluminum foil or waxed paper underneath your fabric.

A natural fabric without nap works best for fabric painting. Nap will cause the lines of your pattern to turn out fuzzy, and some synthetic fabrics have a sizing that will not absorb paint. It is wise to paint a scrap of the fabric, wash and dry it, and check the results before proceeding with the entire project.

A single small brush is enough to begin fabric painting. You may want to add larger brushes later. Good brushes are expensive, but are well worth the money.

To set the paint, iron the finished work on the wrong side of the fabric. Although we have had good luck washing projects in hot water, we suggest that as a precautionary measure you wash fabric painted projects in a cold water cycle.

Embroidery

Cotton embroidery thread contains 6 strands which can be easily separated. The fewer strands you use, the smaller needle you need, the more stitches you will take, and the finer the finished work.

To avoid knotting the thread at the beginning of embroidery, work a running stitch on the surface, positioning it so that subsequent stitches will cover it. Finish a length of thread by running the end under the last few stitches. Always use an embroidery hoop to hold your fabric while you work. We also suggest that you shrink your fabric.

One or two strands of embroidery thread can be threaded easily if you moisten them first. When using more than 2 strands (or large yarn), fold one over the eye of the needle. Pinch the fold tightly between the thumb and forefinger and pull the needle out. Still holding the tightly pinched fold, thread the eye of the needle down over it. When the fold is threaded, you can pull the rest of the yarn through easily.

Illustrations for each of the embroidery stitches are given on the next page. With a little practice even a beginner can produce stitches that are smooth and uniform. Press the completed embroidery work on the wrong side using a steam iron.

Appliqué

An appliqué is a small piece of fabric sewn over a larger background piece.

Mark the complete design on the background fabric. Cut pattern pieces for each portion of the design, adding a seam allowance around the piece. Omit the seam allowance if you use iron-on fusing material.

Stitch just outside the design outline. Turn the seam allowance and stitching to the wrong side of the fabric. Clip the curves in the seam allowance. (See "Clipping Seams," page 6.) Press the appliqué piece flat using a steam iron. Pin and slipstitch the appliqués in place on the background fabric.

To use iron-on fusing material, cut a matching piece of fusing for each of the appliqué pieces. Place the fusing between the appliqué and the background and press with an iron, following the manufacturer's directions to fuse the 2 pieces together. Finish the outer edges with an embroidery stitch.

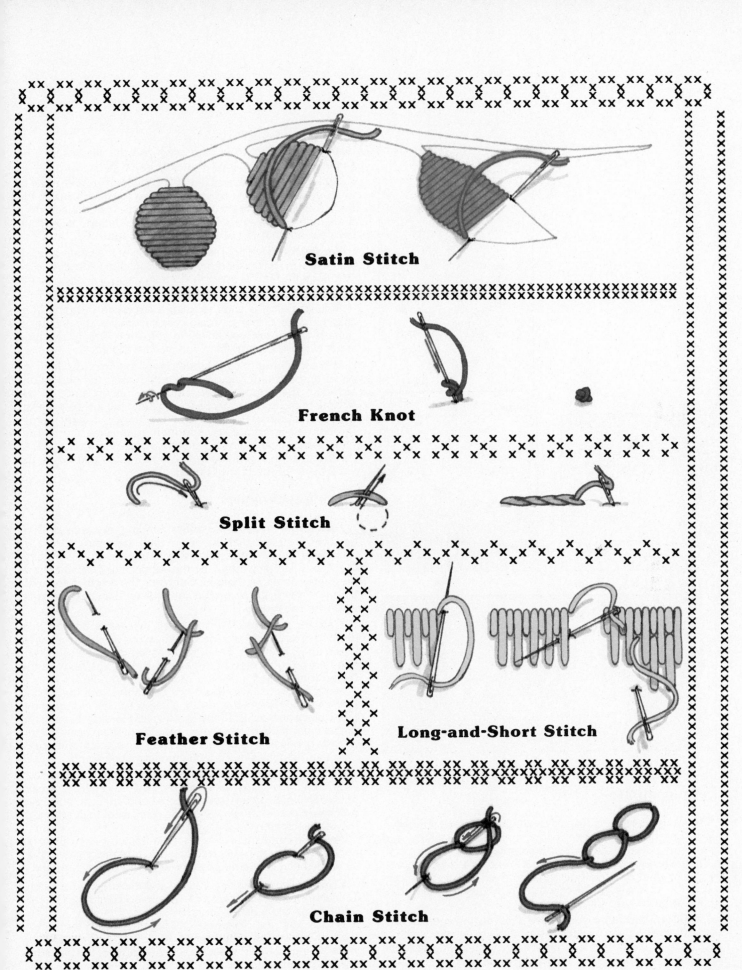

Satin Stitch

French Knot

Split Stitch

Feather Stitch

Long-and-Short Stitch

Chain Stitch

Figure A

Figure B

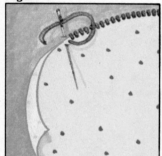

Figure C

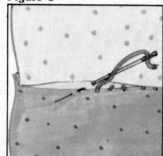

Figure D

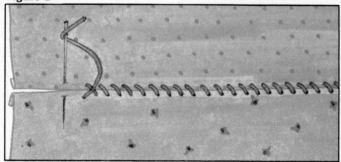

Sewing stitches

Basting stitches are used to hold fabric in place temporarily before the final stitching is done by hand or machine, and are removed after the project is completed.

To baste, take a stitch through the fabric layers, skip a space and take another stitch. Basting stitches are usually fairly long (about ½ inch in length). For easy removal, use a thread color that will be easy to see **(Figure A)**.

Appliqué stitches (overhand stitches) are the equivalent of the embroidered satin stitch. The stitches are perpendicular to the edge of the fabric. The needle is inserted into the fabric directly across from the last stitch and then brought out

diagonally to begin the next stitch. All the stitches are the same length, and spaced evenly **(Figure B)**.

Slipstitching is also called "blindstitching" and is used to invisibly sew one edge to another. Insert the needle inside the folded edge of the fabric. Keep the needle inside the fold for the length of one stitch. Bring the needle out and take a tiny invisible stitch in the other fabric side **(Figure C)**.

Topstitching is a final stitch on the top of the fabric where it will show on the finished project. The stitching line should be very straight, and a uniform distance from the edge of the fabric.

Staystitching is used to keep a cut piece of fabric from stretching out of shape, and to keep cut edge from raveling on pattern pieces not yet sewn. To staystitch, simply machine stitch along the seam line ¼ inch from the edge.

Whipstitching joins 2 fabric pieces together, catching an equal amount of fabric on each edge. Insert the needle underneath the bottom edge. Bring the needle through the bottom fabric and diagonally forward into the top edge. Insert the needle down through the top edge, straight across through the bottom edge, and then up through the bottom edge. Each stitch is worked straight across perpendicularly to the fabric edges, resulting in a diagonal stitch pattern on the visible side of the fabric **(Figure D)**.

Sewing techniques

Bias strips are used for ruffles, binding, or cording. They have more stretch than fabric cut with the grain.

To determine the bias, fold the yardage diagonally, bringing the 2 raw straight edges of the fabric together to form a 45-degree angle on the fold. Cut along the length of the fold, then cut bias strips along the cut foldline; 2 inches is a good width for most uses.

Gathers are used wherever soft fullness is desired in a finished project, and may be done by hand or with a machine. Use a large stitch and sew 1 row of stitching close to the cut edge on the right side of the fabric, leaving the ends of the thread long. Stitch a second row close to the first.

Working on the wrong side of the fabric, pull the 2 long threads gently. Work the resulting gathers to the center of the fabric piece and adjust them evenly over that side. Repeat the process, working from the opposite side of the piece. Pull the threads gently to avoid breaking them. Use heavy-duty sewing thread when gathering heavy weights of fabric.

Clipping seams is necessary on curves or corners so the finished project will lie flat when pressed. To eliminate excess seam allowance on an outward curve or corner, cut v-shaped notches in the seam allowance. Be careful not to cut through the seam stitching.

An inside curve must also be clipped, since there will not be enough fabric in the seam allowance to turn the curve. Clip as close to the stitching as possible without cutting through.

Cording is used for decoration, and to strengthen a seam. To make cording, use cotton cable cord and bias strips slightly longer than the finished length.

Fold a bias strip (wrong sides together) over the cotton cord, matching the long raw edges. Use the zipper foot on your sewing machine to sew down the length of the bias strip, securing the cording inside.

THE TOY CHEST
children's toys and furnishings

Projects In This Section:

Mother Goose

This delightful stuffed terrycloth character can be a decorative and cheerful addition to any child's room — or tuck a brick inside and use her as a unique doorstop.

Figure A

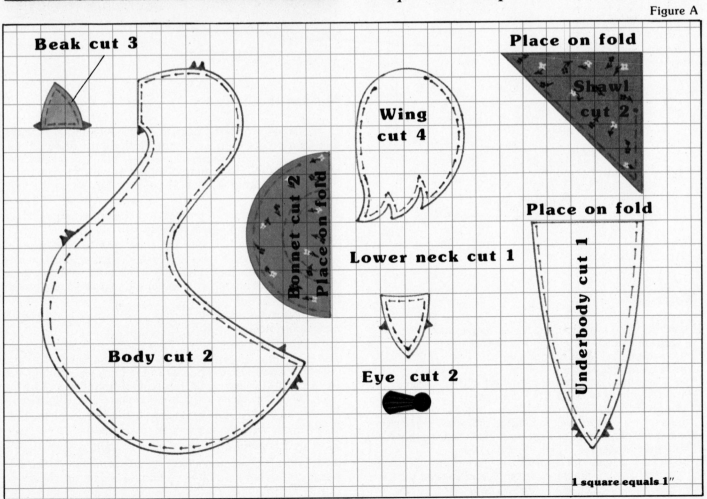

Beak cut 3

Place on fold

Shawl cut 2

Wing cut 4

Bonnet cut 2 Place on fold

Place on fold

Underbody cut 1

Lower neck cut 1

Body cut 2

Eye cut 2

1 square equals 1″

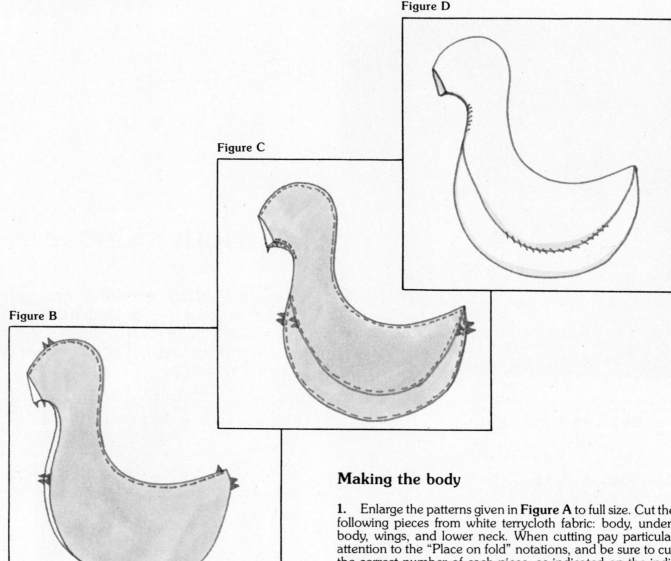

Figure D

Figure C

Figure B

Making the body

1. Enlarge the patterns given in **Figure A** to full size. Cut the following pieces from white terrycloth fabric: body, underbody, wings, and lower neck. When cutting pay particular attention to the "Place on fold" notations, and be sure to cut the correct number of each piece, as indicated on the individual pattern.

2. Pin 2 body pieces right sides together, matching notches. Machine stitch along back **(Figure B)**.

3. Matching notches, pin and then stitch underbody between 2 body pieces with right sides together, as shown in **Figure C**. If you plan to put a brick inside for use as a doorstop, leave a large opening in the middle of one underbody seam.

4. Pin and then stitch lower neck between 2 body pieces, matching notches.

5. Clip corners and curves. Turn the assembled body right side out. If you are inserting a brick, stuff the top portion and tail of the body firmly. Then wrap the brick with batting and place it on the bottom of the goose. Finish stuffing around the brick, then whipstitch the bottom opening closed **(Figure D)**.

6. Stuff the head and neck tightly, working through the hole in the neck. Whipstitch the neck hole closed.

7. Cut 3 beak pieces from the orange felt.

8. Pin the 3 beak pieces right sides together along the side seams, matching notches. Machine stitch as shown in **Figure E**.

Materials

1 yard of white terrycloth fabric, 36 inches wide.
¼ yard of 36-inch-wide orange calico fabric.
4-inch-square piece of orange felt.
3-inch-square piece of black felt.
5-inch length of ¼ inch (or narrower) elastic.
1¾ yards of yellow baby-sized rick-rack.
2 pounds of polyester quilt batting.
1 brick (if you plan to use the finished project as a doorstop).
Sewing needle; white, orange, and black sewing thread.
1 wire coathanger.
The tools you need are: wire clippers to cut the coathanger, pliers, sewing machine, scissors, and straight pins.
Dressmaker's carbon paper, tracing paper, and pencil.

Figure E

Figure F

Figure I

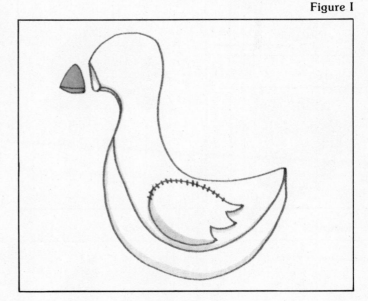

Figure G

Figure H

9. Clip curves. Turn right side out and press as shown in **Figure F.** Stuff the beak tightly with batting.

10. Pin 2 wing pieces right sides together. Stitch along seam lines, leaving the seam unstitched between the small circles **(Figure G)**.

11. Clip corners and curves. Turn right side out and press. Stuff lightly, turn raw edges to the inside, and whipstitch the opening closed as shown in **Figure H.**

12. Repeat steps 10 and 11 to complete the remaining wing.

13. Turn the raw edges of the beak to the inside. Fit the beak over the opening in the head front and whipstitch it in place **(Figure I)**.

14. Whipstitch the wings in place on both sides of the body.

15. Cut 2 eyes from black felt. Hand tack them in place with needle and thread as shown in **Figure J**.

Making the cap and shawl

1. Cut 2 hat pieces and 2 shawl pieces from orange calico fabric.

Figure J

Figure K

Figure M

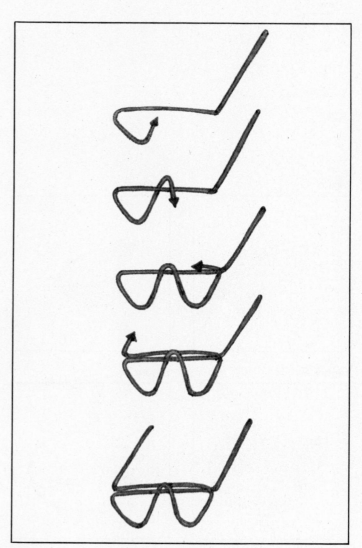

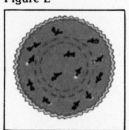

Figure L

Figure N

Figure O

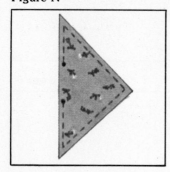

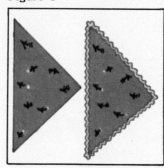

Figure P

6. Pull the ends of the elastic until it gathers the cap. Place the cap on the head and adjust the gathers until it fits. Sew the ends of the elastic together tightly as shown in **Figure M.** Cut off excess elastic and pull it back inside the casing. Whipstitch the opening of the casing closed.

7. Pin the 2 shawl pieces right sides together. Machine stitch seams, leaving an opening between the small circles (**Figure N**).

8. Clip corners, turn right side out and press. Topstitch around all edges. Sew rick-rack around all edges as shown in **Figure O.**

9. Tie shawl around the neck.

Making the glasses

1. To make the glasses, bend a coathanger with a pair of pliers, following the steps shown in **Figure P.** The exact size of the glasses is not critical, but at each step, check the fit on your completed goose.

2. Hand tack the glasses in place over the beak and on both sides of the head underneath the bonnet.

2. Pin the 2 hat pieces right sides together. Stitch the outer edges, leaving unstitched between the small circles (**Figure K**).

3. Clip the seam and turn the hat right side out. Turn the remaining raw edges to the inside and press.

4. Pin and then topstitch rick-rack around the outer edges as shown in **Figure L.**

5. Topstitch over both of the casing lines. To insert the elastic, make a small slit in one layer of fabric between the 2 casing stitching lines. Insert the elastic through the casing between the 2 fabric layers.

Figure A

1 square equals 1"

Honeybears

Endearing faces and soft bodies of these cuddly bears will charm children and grownups alike. You'll want to stitch up all 3 members of this bear-y loveable family.

Materials

To make Momma, Poppa and Baby Honeybears you will need a total of 2½ yards of white cotton fabric.

The clothing on each of the bears can also be cut from scraps of fabric on hand, and are not limited to the colors shown. Simply match the size of the fabric to the clothes portion of the bear after you enlarge the pattern. The clothing may also be fabric painted, using artist's acrylic paints (red, blue, yellow, white, and black) and a small brush.

The bears' facial features can be either embroidered (use scraps of cotton embroidery thread) or you can use permanent markers or fabric paint to complete them.

Odds and ends of ribbon, lace, or seam tape for tying bows on Momma and Baby Bear.

Scissors and straight pins.

Sewing machine (or they may be completed by hand).

Quilt batting (or other stuffing).

Carbon paper, soft pencil, needle and white thread.

Figure B

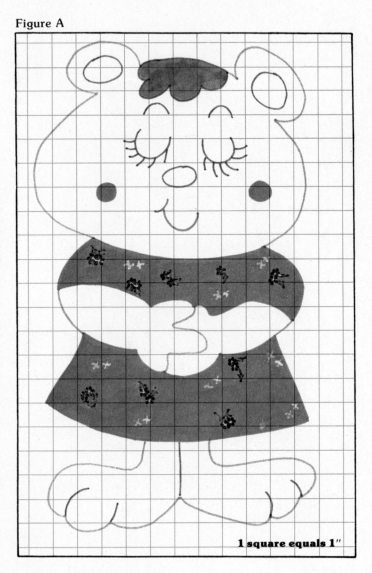

Figure A

Figure A

1 square equals 1"

1 square equals 1"

Cutting the patterns

1. Enlarge the back and front view for each of the 3 Honeybears (**Figure A, pages 13, 14 and 15**) to full size.

2. Transfer the full-size pattern to white cotton fabric using a soft pencil and carbon paper, adding a ½-inch seam allowance around each of the pattern pieces.

3. Cut out each of the resulting pattern pieces.

Sewing the body

1. Pin the fabric front and back of each bear right sides together.

2. Sew along the outer pattern lines, leaving the top of the head (between the ears) open to allow for turning and stuffing (**Figure B**).

3. Trim and clip all seams, cutting carefully up to the stitching at all corners and curves.

4. Turn the bear right side out and press gently with a steam iron.

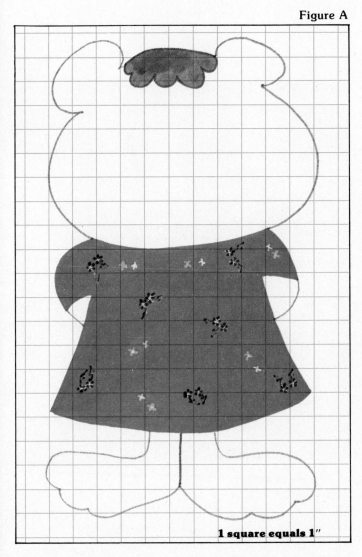

1 square equals 1"

5. Stuff lightly, but firmly with fiberfill or batting, and whip-stitch the opening together. A knitting needle is helpful to poke stuffing into toes and corners.

Appliqué

If you intend to complete the bears entirely in fabric paint or markers and then add the embroidery, skip this appliqué section and go the the "Fabric Painting and Embroidery" section.

1. Cut the clothing sections from the full-size body patterns which you have enlarged. Place the individual pieces on appropriate sizes of fabric and cut out, adding a ¼-inch hem allowance around each of the fabric pieces.

2. Staystitch around the outer pattern lines of each of the fabric clothing pieces. Turn the ¼-inch hem allowance to the wrong side of the fabric.

3. Pin the pressed clothing piece on the bear body matching the pattern lines, and pin in place. Whipstitch around the edges to hold it securely. More detailed instructions on appliqué are given in the "Tips and Techniques" section of this book.

Fabric painting and embroidery

If you have appliquéd the clothing, skip step 1 and go to step 2.

1. When painting the clothing, we suggest that you paint the background first with a continuous tone in a fairly light color. Let the background dry thoroughly. Add a pattern to the fabric, if you wish. Then add all clothing details such as collars and cuffs.

2. Paint or embroider the leg and toe outlines and the facial features. Suggested colors are indicated in Figure A. Directions for embroidery stitches and fabric painting are given in the "Tips and Techniques" section at the front of this book.

3. To finish, tie bows on the ears of both Momma and Baby Honeybear.

Figure A

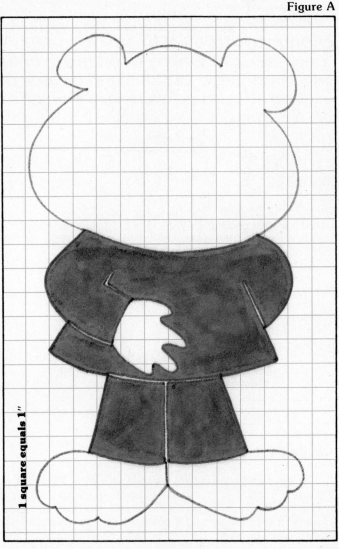

1 square equals 1"

15

Schoolhouse Diaper Bag

The inside of this diaper bag is large enough to tote all of baby's or toddler's "necessaries." On the outside are dolls and playthings, buttons and lacings to occupy little ones in a doctor's office or on shopping expeditions.

Materials

1½ yards of 36-inch-wide canvas fabric.
54-inch length of 36-inch-wide bonded polyester fiberfill.
1½ yards of 36-inch-wide red calico cotton fabric for the lining.
¼ yard of 36-inch-wide bright green calico cotton fabric for the shutter.
Two 4 x 6-inch pieces of yellow calico fabric for the front door.
1 pair of white shoestrings (to fit 3- or 4-eyelet shoes).
3 large snaps.
One ¾-inch-diameter button.
4 small nylon fastener "spots."
Fabric paint or artist's acrylic paint in the following colors: red, blue, yellow, white, and black.
Artist's fine paint brush.
Thread, scissors, straight pins, and sewing machine.
Dressmaker's carbon paper, tracing paper, and pencil.

Cutting the pieces

1. Enlarge and transfer the patterns shown in **Figure A** to full size. Transfer each of the enlarged patterns (with the exception of the Shutter and Door) to the canvas fabric. Leave 2 inches between the pattern pieces to allow for later hemming.

2. Paint each of the transferred patterns with acrylic paint following the suggested colors indicated in Figure A.

3. Allow the painted patterns to dry overnight.

4. Place a damp cloth over the painted pieces and press with a hot iron. This will set the paint. Remember to protect underneath the painted piece with aluminum foil or waxed paper.

Sewing the individual pieces

1. Each of the individual pieces is lined and stuffed separately, then sewn together to form the finished diaper bag. Cut each of the painted patterns out, leaving a ½-inch seam allowance on all sides of each pattern.

2. Cut a piece of lining fabric the exact size of the Front, Back, 2 Sides, Roof, and Bottom.

3. Pin the pattern piece and matching lining right sides together and machine stitch around all edges along the outer pattern lines, leaving an opening large enough to turn and insert the inner lining.

4. Follow steps 2 and 3 for the Tree, Boy, and Girl pattern pieces, backing them with the canvas fabric rather than the lining fabric.

5. Clip corners and curves on each of the pattern pieces and turn them right side out.

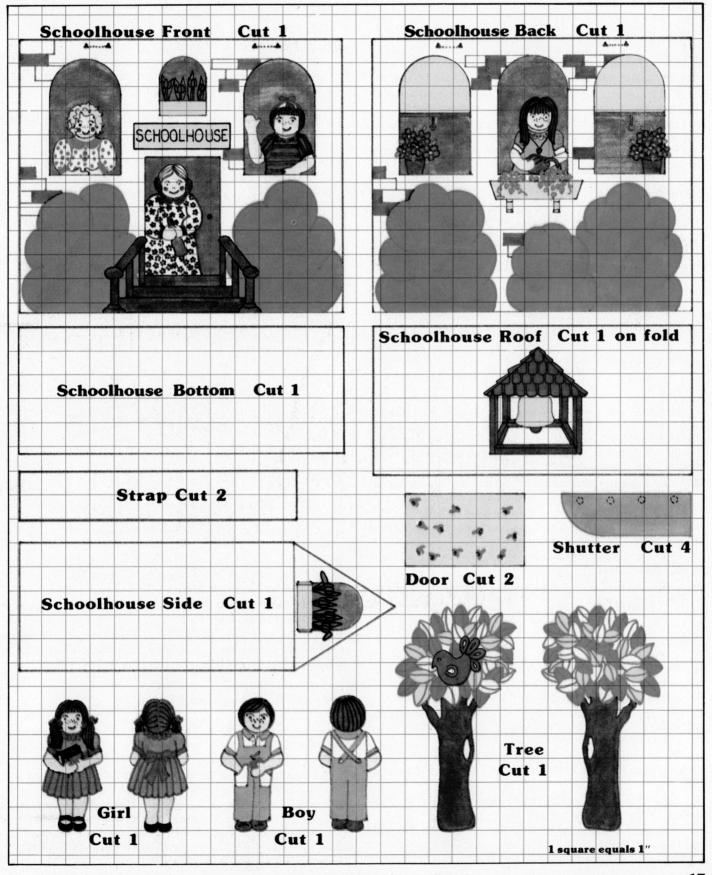

Schoolhouse Front   Cut 1

Schoolhouse Back   Cut 1

SCHOOLHOUSE

Schoolhouse Bottom   Cut 1

Schoolhouse Roof   Cut 1 on fold

Strap Cut 2

Schoolhouse Side   Cut 1

Door   Cut 2

Shutter   Cut 4

Girl
Cut 1

Boy
Cut 1

Tree
Cut 1

1 square equals 1"

6. Press the turned pieces with a steam iron. Turn the remaining raw edges of the opening to the inside and press.

7. Cut a piece of bonded polyester fiberfill slightly smaller than the size of each of the turned pieces.

8. Insert the fiberfill through the opening in the turned piece and smooth it so it is flat. Pin in place. On the Bottom piece you may wish to add an additional piece of heavy buckram for extra strength and support.

Figure B   **Figure C**

9. Topstitch through all thicknesses (painted top, fiberfill, and lining) ⅜ inch from the edge of all of the larger pieces (Sides, Front, Back, Bottom, and Roof). To add extra stability, double stitch around each of the painted windows, doors, bushes, and around the belfry on the Roof.

10. Cut 4 Shutter pieces from the bright green cotton fabric, and 2 Door pieces from the yellow calico fabric.

11. Sew 2 of the Shutter pieces right sides together, leaving a small opening. Turn and stuff as you did previously. Repeat for the remaining pair of shutters.

12. Follow the same procedure to sew, turn and stuff the 2 Door pattern pieces.

13. Stitch ⅛ inch from the edge around each of the Shutters and the Door.

Adding the trim

1. Carefully poke holes in each of the completed shutters where indicated on the pattern and work a buttonhole stitch (or zig-zag machine stitch) around each of the holes.

2. Pin the shutters on the front windows as shown in the photograph, and machine stitch down the straight portion of the outer edges, securing them to the front.

3. Work a buttonhole on the completed door to correspond with the button placement indicated on the front of the diaper bag.

4. Sew the door in place. Sew a button on the doorway where indicated on the pattern.

5. Sew one side of a snap on the back of the tree, boy and girl. Sew the other side of the snap to the corresponding position on the diaper bag side and front.

Roof Assembly

1. Sew along the solid line down the center of the Roof. Fold the Roof in half lengthwise along the stitching line with the lining to the inside. Pin in place.

2. Sew through the double roof thickness ¼ inch from the previous stitching.

3. To form a peak, stitch another parallel stitching line 1 inch from the second stitching as shown in **Figure B.**

Figure D   **Figure E**

Figure F

Final Assembly

1. Pin the left and right sides of the schoolhouse to the front along the side seams (**Figure C**). Sew both seams, stitching over the previous topstitching. The seams will be on the outside.

2. Pin the schoolhouse back to both sides and sew over the topstitching as you did for the front (**Figure D**). Again, the seams will be on the outside.

3. Turn the assembly upside-down, pin the bottom in place and stitch (**Figure E**).

4. Pin the roof to the top of the schoolhouse with the belfry facing the front of the schoolhouse. Sew the roof to the front only, leaving the back open for access to the inside.

Adding the straps and finishing

1. Fold one Strap in half lengthwise and press (**Figure F**). Turn the raw edges to the inside until the strap measures 1 inch wide. Press with a steam iron. Topstitch the open edge.

2. Pin and sew the straps to the front and back of the schoolhouse where indicated on the pattern.

3. Sew nylon fastener "spots" to hold the roof in place. Sew one "spot" to the top of each of the schoolhouse sides at the top of the peak, and to corresponding positions on the roof. Sew nylon fasteners to the top of the schoolhouse back and to corresponding positions inside the schoolhouse roof.

Amy Rag Doll

This cuddly rag doll will brighten the eyes of your special child. Her fabric body is soft and huggable, and fits perfectly in a little girl's arms.

Materials

¾ yard of white (or flesh-colored) cotton fabric for the doll body.
½ yard of yellow calico for dress.
½ yard of pink cotton for apron.
¼ yard white cotton or cotton eyelet for pantalettes.
Polyester quilt batting or other stuffing material.
Blue, brown, and pink cotton embroidery thread.
¼ yard of ¼-inch-wide elastic.
12-inch-square piece of black calico fabric.
1 skein of medium-weight brown yarn and needle large enough to accommodate 1 strand of yarn.
1 package of yellow rick-rack.
1 small snap, straight pins, and sewing needle.
Sewing thread to match fabrics.
Scissors, iron, and ironing board.
Dressmaker's carbon paper, tracing paper, and pencil.

Cutting the pattern

1.   Enlarge the patterns given in **Figure A** to full size.

2.   Pin the full-size pattern to the appropriate color of fabric and cut out each one. Pay particular attention to the "place on fold" notations, and be sure to cut the number of pieces specified on each pattern.

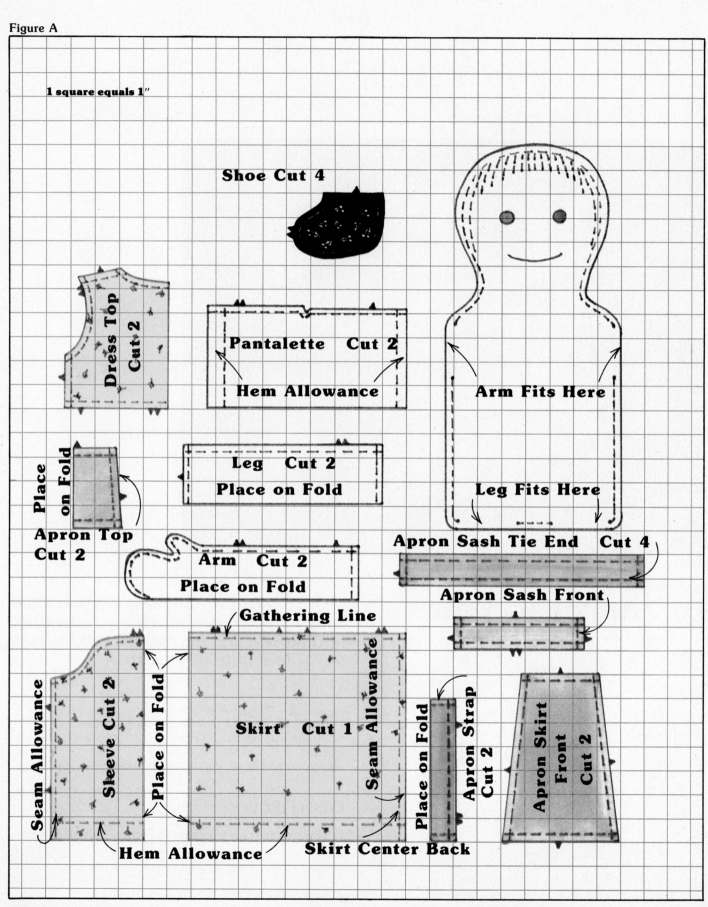

1 square equals 1″

Shoe Cut 4

Dress Top Cut 2

Pantalette Cut 2

Hem Allowance

Arm Fits Here

Leg Fits Here

Place on Fold

Apron Top Cut 2

Leg Cut 2 Place on Fold

Arm Cut 2 Place on Fold

Apron Sash Tie End Cut 4

Apron Sash Front

Gathering Line

Seam Allowance

Sleeve Cut 2

Place on Fold

Skirt Cut 1

Seam Allowance

Place on Fold

Apron Strap Cut 2

Apron Skirt Front Cut 2

Hem Allowance

Skirt Center Back

Figure B

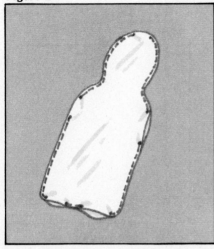

Figure C

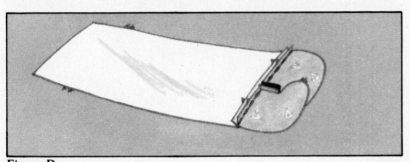

Figure D

Figure E

Figure F

Figure G

Sewing the body

1. Place the 2 Body pieces right sides together and sew a ½-inch seam, leaving an opening between the small circles for legs, arms, and at the top of the head **(Figure B).**

2. Clip curves, and turn the body right side out. Turn the raw edges to the inside on all 5 openings, and press gently with a steam iron. Stuff the body firmly with batting.

3. Sew 2 Shoe pieces right sides together between the small circles **(Figure C).**

4. Sew the bottom of the Leg piece to the shoe tops, placing the shoe seam in the center of the leg **(Figure D).**

5. Fold Leg piece right sides together and sew down the back of leg and around the shoe. Leave the top of the leg open and unstitched **(Figure E).** Clip curves, turn right side out, and press. Stuff the combined leg and shoe.

6. Repeat steps 3 through 5 to make the second leg and shoe.

7. Fold one Arm piece right sides together and sew down the side seam and around the hand **(Figure F).** Clip curves, turn right side out, press and stuff with batting. Repeat for the remaining arm.

8. Pin the arms, with thumbs up, inside arm openings on body, and topstitch them in place **(Figure G).**

9. Press the leg so the toe points to the front and the leg seams are at the center back. Pin the legs inside the openings on the lower body. Topstitch them in place.

10. Whipstitch the opening at the top of the head together.

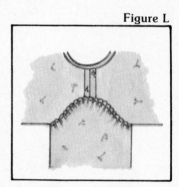

Figure L

Figure M

Figure H

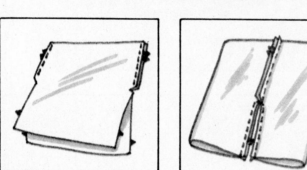

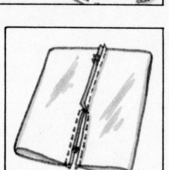

Figure I

Figure J

The facial features and hair

1. Embroider the eyes (blue) using the satin stitch. Embroider the mouth (pink) using the split stitch. Illustrated instructions for these stitches are given in the "Tips and Techniques" section at the beginning of this book.

2. Attach the hair along the dashes marked on the head pattern. Thread the needle with an 18-inch length of yarn. Pull the yarn through the fabric and tie **(Figure H)**. For long hair, leave both tie ends long. We tied the hair in ponytails on both sides of the head. For shorter hair, use shorter lengths of yarn.

Sewing the pantalettes and dress

1. Place 2 Pantalette pieces right sides together and sew the center front and center back seams **(Figure I)**.

2. Refold the stitched pantalettes, matching center front and center back seams. Sew center leg seams **(Figure J)**.

3. Sew a ⅜-inch hem around the bottom of the pantalette legs and around the waist. Install narrow elastic at the waist. Add lace around the bottom leg hems, if desired.

4. Pin 2 Dress Top pieces right sides together and sew the shoulder seams. Slit the center back 2 inches deep and hem the resulting raw edges **(Figure K)**.

5. Turn the raw edges on the neckline to the inside and topstitch. Add lace around the neckline, if desired. Sew a small snap at the top of the neckline back opening.

6. Gather the curve of the top sleeve and pin it to the armhole in the dress top, easing the gathers to fit **(Figure L)**. Hem the sleeve bottom and add lace or rick-rack trim, if desired. Repeat for the remaining sleeve.

7. Sew the underarm and side seams on the dress top **(Figure M)**.

8. Turn up a ½-inch hem allowance on the skirt and stitch **(Figure N)**. Add lace or rick-rack to the bottom, if desired.

9. Gather the skirt along the top edge, leaving center back seam allowances ungathered. Sew the skirt right sides together along the center back seam.

10. Matching notches, sew the skirt to the dress top (right sides together), easing the skirt gathers to fit.

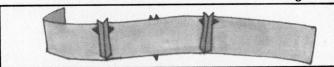
Figure O

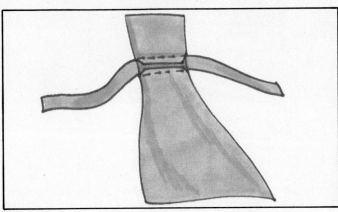

Figure Q

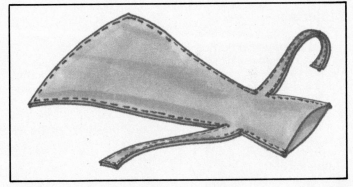

Figure P

Sewing the apron

1. Sew 2 Apron Sash Tie Ends to 1 Apron Sash Front and press seams open **(Figure O)**.

2. Matching notches and with right sides together, sew the Apron Top and Apron Skirt to the center of the Apron Sash Front. Clip seams at all 4 corners and press, as shown in **Figure P.**

3. Repeat steps 1 and 2 for the remaining apron pieces (2 Sash Tie Ends, 1 Sash Front, Top, and Skirt).

4. Pin the assembled apron sides right sides together, and sew around all edges, leaving only the top seam allowance open and unstitched **(Figure Q).** Clip corners and turn right side out. Press the top unstitched seam allowance to the inside.

5. Fold 2 Apron Strap pieces right sides together. Sew along 3 sides, leaving 1 narrow end open. Turn and press.

6. Pin the open end of the Apron straps to either side of the unstitched apron top, as shown in **Figure R.** Topstitch across apron top to secure.

7. Dress the doll, hand tack the apron straps in place at the back, and tie the apron in a bow in back.

Figure R

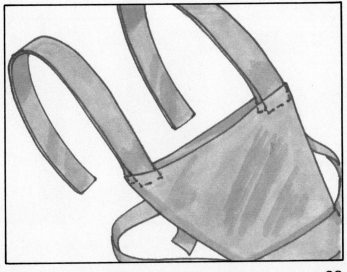

Card Table Playhouse

All little kids love a playhouse, and this one will be a real favorite with Mom, too. It fits over a card table so when playtime is over, it can be folded up and put away in the closet.

Materials

1 yard of calico fabric (for curtains) 36 inches wide.
½ yard of orange felt, 36 inches wide.
½ yard of lime green felt, 36 inches wide. (In addition to this yardage, add the felt necessary for the roof, which will be figured below).
1½ yards bright green felt, 36 inches wide.
Background fabric (yardage also figured below). Any heavy fabric will do.
Sewing thread.
Oatmeal box.
12 medium-sized snaps.
Dressmaker's carbon paper, tracing paper, and pencil.

Cardboard box, approximately 11½ x 17 inches and 9½ inches tall; any similar size will work.
Several large books or something heavy to use as a weight.
1 package (3 yards) of seam tape the same color as the background (optional).
To make the chimney bird you will need: a piece of calico fabric 11 x 18 inches for the bird's body, and felt scraps for the wings. The eyes may be buttons or may be cut from felt. You need a small amount of quilt batting or other stuffing material.
To figure the amount of background fabric needed for your card table, complete the steps in **Figure B**.

Figure A

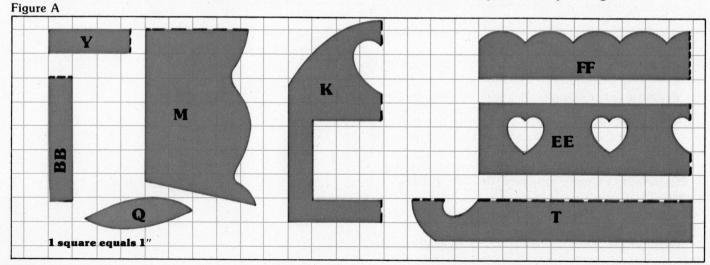

1 square equals 1"

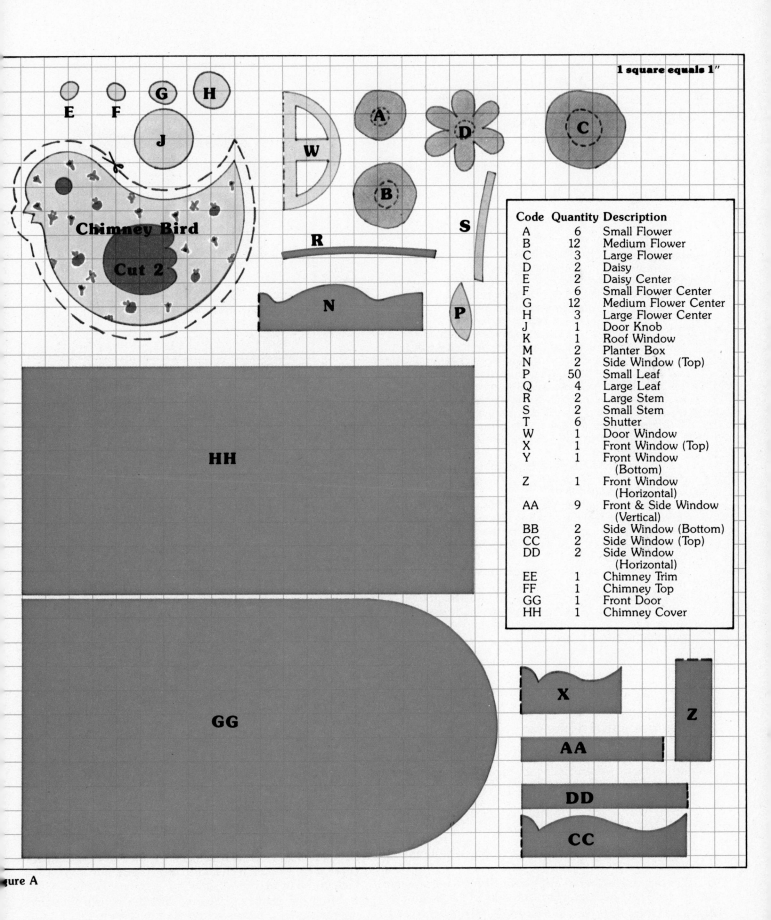

1 square equals 1″

E · F · G · H

J

Chimney Bird

Cut 2

W · A · B · D · C

R · S · P

N

HH

GG

X · Z

AA

DD

CC

Code	Quantity	Description
A	6	Small Flower
B	12	Medium Flower
C	3	Large Flower
D	2	Daisy
E	2	Daisy Center
F	6	Small Flower Center
G	12	Medium Flower Center
H	3	Large Flower Center
J	1	Door Knob
K	1	Roof Window
M	2	Planter Box
N	2	Side Window (Top)
P	50	Small Leaf
Q	4	Large Leaf
R	2	Large Stem
S	2	Small Stem
T	6	Shutter
W	1	Door Window
X	1	Front Window (Top)
Y	1	Front Window (Bottom)
Z	1	Front Window (Horizontal)
AA	9	Front & Side Window (Vertical)
BB	2	Side Window (Bottom)
CC	2	Side Window (Top)
DD	2	Side Window (Horizontal)
EE	1	Chimney Trim
FF	1	Chimney Top
GG	1	Front Door
HH	1	Chimney Cover

Figure A

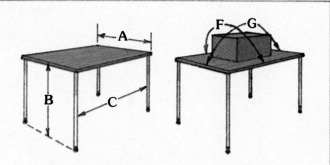

1. Card table top (side to side) = _____ inches + 2 inches = *(Measurement A)*.
2. Card table height (floor to table top) = _____ inches + 2 inches = *(Measurement B)*.
3. Card table width (from end to end) = _____ inches + 2 inches = *(Measurement C)*.

If Measurement A is 36 inches or less, then you will be figuring yardage based on 36-inch-wide fabric. If Measurement A is over 36 inches, you will need to purchase 45-inch-wide fabric. We assume that in no case will Measurement A exceed 45 inches. Complete the following, using the figures which you just filled in above.

(Measurement B) × 4 = *(Measurement D)*
(Measurement D) + *(Measurement A)* = *(Measurement E)*
(Measurement E) ÷ 12 = *(number of feet of fabric)* ÷ 3 = *(Number of yards of fabric required for your table)*

To figure "roof" fabric, place a cardboard box on top of the card table. Beginning at one edge of the table, measure over the top of the box to the opposite edge of the table. Add 8 inches, and that will be *Measurement F.*

Perform the same measurement across the box using the remaining 2 sides. Add 8 inches to that, and you have Measurement G. (Measurement F) x (Measurement G) is the size piece of lime green felt you need for the roof. If you can't find felt wide enough, it is fine to piece it.

Figure B

Cutting the pattern pieces

1. Enlarge the pattern pieces shown in **Figure A,** then cut out each of them. When cutting, be sure to cut the quantity specified and to use the correct color of fabric.

Sewing the sides and top

When completing this section, refer to your measurements in Figure B.

1. Cut 4 House Sides *(Measurement B)* by *(Measurement C)*. These will be the front, back, and sides of the playhouse.
2. Cut 1 House Top *(Measurement A)* by *(Measurement C)*.

26

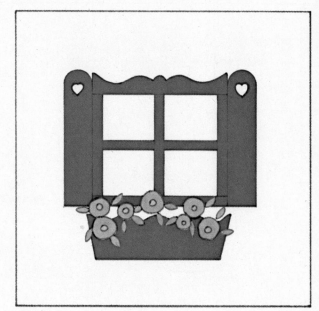

Figure C

3. Sew a 1-inch hem on the side and bottom edges of all 4 House Side pieces. Leave the top edge unsewn.
4. Lay one hemmed House Side piece on a flat surface. The top edge should be unhemmed. Place the felt pieces on the background House Side piece with the window centered. When you have the arrangement you desire, pin the felt pieces securely **(Figure C)**.
5. Machine or hand stitch each piece of felt to the background fabric, as close to the outer edges of the felt as possible. Double stitch around all of the window pieces. Cut out the window "panes."
6. Repeat the procedure (steps 4 and 5) for the other House Side.
7. Construct the House Front in the same manner **(Figure D)**. If your house is wider than shown, leave more space between the window and the front door.
8. After all of the felt is sewn in place, triple stitch the front door. Then triple stitch again about ¼ inch from the first stitching line. Cut the door "open" with scissors as shown in Figure D. Machine stitch across the 2 stitching lines just above the cutting line to avoid tearing. Cut out the front window "panes." No work is required on the back of the house, as it is left plain.

Making the curtains

1. Cut 6 pieces of calico fabric for the curtains, each measuring 10 x 18 inches.
2. Sew a ½-inch hem in each of the two 18-inch sides **(Figure E)**. Sew a 2-inch hem in one 10-inch side **(Figure F)**. Gather the other 10-inch side.
3. Pull the gathering threads until the curtain measures approximately 5 inches across the top **(Figure G)**.

Figure D

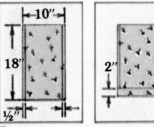

Figure E

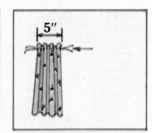

Figure F

Figure G

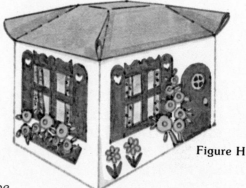

Figure H

4. Pin 2 hemmed curtains to the inside of each window. Double stitch along the gathering line.

House assembly

1. Place the House Top (which you have not used) on top of the card table and center it with the right side of the fabric against the table top. Place a weight on top.

2. With wrong sides facing out and the raw edge at the top, pin the House Sides, Front, and Back to the House Top. The pinned seam will be on the outside. Check to make sure that all the sides are an even length. Remove the entire assembly and machine stitch the pinned seams. Double stitch for strength. Press the seams, turn the house right side out, and replace it over the card table.

3. An optional step at this point is to sew lengths of seam binding to opposite sides of the house at all 4 corners. They may then be tied to keep the corners together.

Making the roof

1. Place the cardboard box in the center of the table, with the short end parallel to the front and back of the house.

2. Center the roof fabric on top of the box. It should overhang the sides, back, and front evenly. Place a weight on top of the roof fabric.

3. Begin at the corner of the box, and draw up and pin all the excess fabric so that the "roof line" is straight from the corner of the box to the corner of the table. Repeat for the other 3 corners **(Figure H)**.

4. Sew all 4 seams, double stitching for strength. Trim seams to ½ inch and press open.

5. Replace the "roof," right side out. First mark and then sew snaps at each of the 4 corners and at 2 places on each side (between the corners).

6. Pin the roof window at the center front of the roof as shown in the photograph at the beginning of these instructions. Sew in place.

7. Cut scallops into the overhanging edge of the roof. Use the Door Window pattern as a scallop guide. Begin in the center back of the roof, cutting all the way around and ending where you began.

Chimney

1. Cover the oatmeal box with the Chimney Cover (HH) which you previously cut from green felt. Tack in place by hand.

2. Wrap the Chimney Top (FF) around the top of the oatmeal box, with the scallops extending just above the box. Tack in place.

3. Wrap the Chimney Trim (EE) around the oatmeal box, covering the bottom edge of the Chimney Top. Tack in place.

Chimney bird

1. Place the bird pattern on a double thickness of fabric. Pin in place and cut out.

2. Place the pieces right sides together and sew along the stitching line, leaving an opening large enough to turn and stuff the bird.

3. Turn the bird right side out, stuff, and blindstitch the opening shut.

4. Cut the wings from felt and whipstitch them to the sides of the bird. Add buttons or felt circles for eyes as shown in the photograph.

Alphabet Coverlet

Made from sheets, this coverlet shows off the ABC's with a matching design for each letter. And its bright primary colors will set a cheerful theme in a child's room.

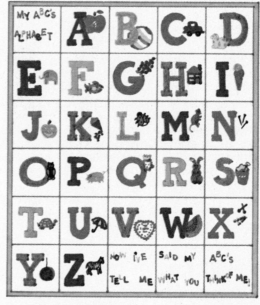

Materials

2 plain white full-size sheets (1 for the quilt front and 1 for the backing.)

Artist's acrylic paints (or fabric paint) in 5 basic colors: red, yellow, blue, black, and white.

2 artist's paint brushes; 1 fine and 1 medium size.

Quilt batting for a full-size quilt. You can generally find batting packaged for making a quilt. Polyester batting is preferable for its washability.

Straight pins, white thread, scissors, yardstick, sewing machine, and pencil.

8 yards of green blanket binding (or pick any other of the paint colors you wish.)

18 yards of red bias binding to outline the alphabet blocks.

To keep the quilt lines as straight as possible, it is helpful to have a T-square or anything that has square corners (a piece of heavy cardboard from the back of a writing tablet, for example.)

You will also need a large flat surface to work on such as a large piece of plywood, a flat floor surface, or a dining table. Be sure to protect the surface so that the paint will not stain it.

Dressmaker's carbon paper, tracing paper, and pencil.

Laying out the design

1. Press both sheets to remove wrinkles and fold lines.

2. Stretch and pin 1 sheet as smoothly as possible on top of your work surface.

3. Use a pencil to rule off the sheet in 13-inch squares as shown in **Figure A.** There should be 5 squares across the top of the sheet and 6 squares down the side for a total of 30 squares. Leave at least 2 inches for a border around the outer edges of the blocks.

Figure A

Transferring the designs

1. Enlarge to full size each of the alphabet designs shown in **Figure B,** pages 29 through 33.

2. Place each of the enlarged designs in their appropriate blocks on the sheet. Exact placement is not necessary as long as both the letter and design fit within the individual block. Figure A shows the general placement of the letters and designs.

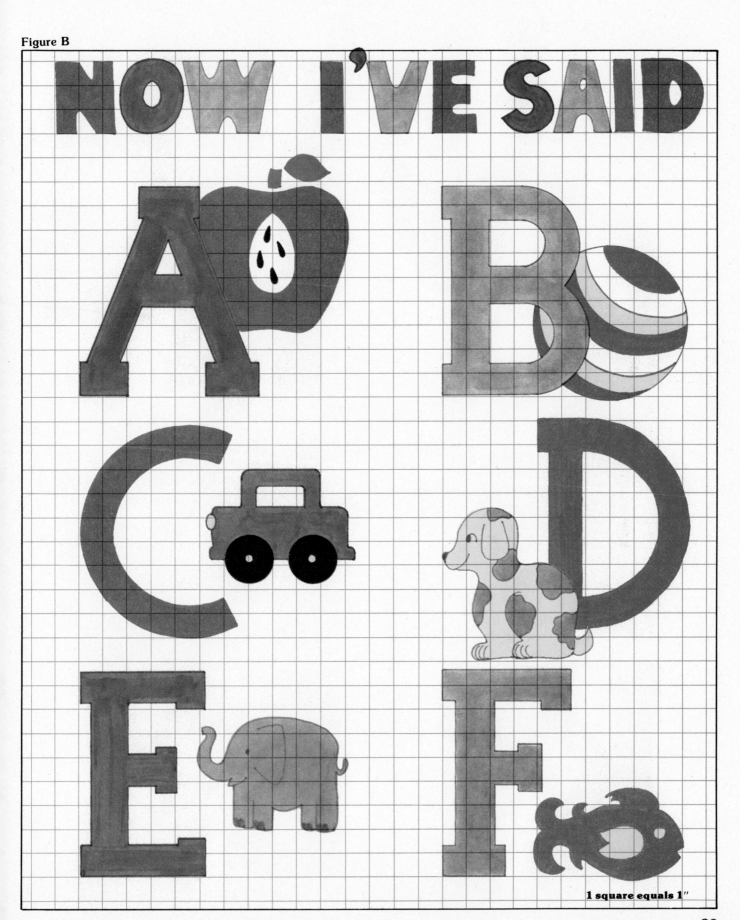

1 square equals 1"

MY ABC'S TELL

1 square equals 1″

ME WHAT YOU

M N

O P

Q R

1 square equals 1″

Figure B

1 square equals 1"

Figure B

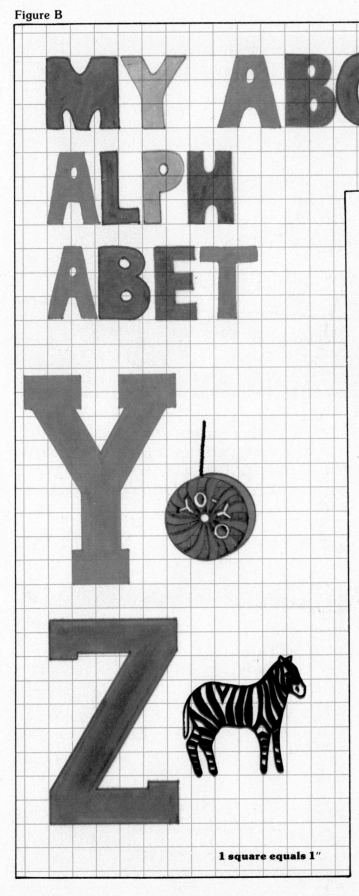

1 square equals 1″

Painting

1. Follow the pattern lines to paint each of the designs. It is a good idea to begin at the top of the quilt and work down to avoid having to place your hands and brushes on already painted work.

2. A suggested color chart is provided in Figure A. However, feel free to change any of the colors you wish to blend with a child's room colors. If you mix a color, make sure you mix enough to complete the portion you are painting, as it is extremely difficult to remix and exactly match colors.

3. When you have finished painting, let the entire work dry overnight.

4. Place a damp cloth over each portion of the finished design (remember to protect underneath) and steam with a medium-hot iron. This will set your design.

5. The quilt can now be washed gently in cold water or dry-cleaned without color loss.

Quilting

1. Lay the remaining sheet (to be used as the quilt backing) on a large flat surface.

2. Place a layer of batting on top of the sheet, making sure it is an even thickness throughout.

3. Place the painted sheet, right side up, on top of the batting.

4. Working from the middle out, smooth and pin the 3 layers together along the straight block lines. Pin at close intervals to make sewing easier.

5. Machine stitch along all penciled block lines. Begin stitching at the center of the quilt and work out to the edges.

6. To set off the blocks, pin bias tape over the stitched block lines and baste in place. Machine stitch on both edges of the bias tape.

7. Again place the quilt on a flat surface. Pin each individual block flat and machine stitch around the outside edges of the letter and design in that block. Repeat the procedure for each of the remaining blocks.

8. Pin and machine stitch the raw outer edges of the quilt, stitching through all 3 layers. Trim away any excess fabric, leaving about 1 inch of fabric all the way around the outer edges.

9. Encase the edges in blanket binding, following the manufacturer's instructions on the package.

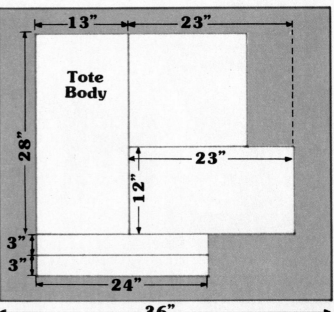

Travel Pal Tote Bag

Pack it with clothes for a youngster's car trip. One side is a pillow for naps; the other side has colorful game squares to occupy children during long trips.

Materials

1 yard of light canvas (or heavy cotton) fabric, 36 inches wide.
¾ yard lining fabric in a small cotton print.
Small amount of polyester fiberfill or quilt batting for stuffing the pillow.
12 medium-sized nylon fasteners or snaps.
Scissors, straight pins, needle and thread, sewing machine, and iron.
Artist's acrylic paint (or fabric paint) in 5 colors: red, blue, yellow, black, and white.
Artist's small paint brush.

Sewing the tote

1. Cut the tote pieces, following the patterns given in **Figure A.**

2. Fold the Tote Body in half lengthwise and sew a ½-inch-wide seam up both sides, as shown in **Figure B.** Turn the Tote Body right side out and press.

3. Sew identical side seams on the Tote Lining; do not turn the lining.

4. Fold the top raw edges under ½ inch on both the Tote Body and the Tote Lining; press.

Figure A

5. Slip the Tote Lining inside the Tote Body and pin them together, as shown in **Figure C.**

6. Cut 2 strap pieces, each 24 x 3 inches. Fold the raw edges to the inside and topstitch along both sides of the straps, as shown in **Figure D.**

7. Pin the straps to the tote, sandwiching them between the Tote Lining and Body, about 2 inches in from the side seams. Topstitch around the top of the tote, securing the tote lining and straps, as shown in **Figure E.**

Cutting and painting

1. Enlarge the patterns for the game squares, as shown in **Figure F.** Transfer them to the canvas fabric, leaving a ½-inch seam allowance on all 4 sides of each square.

2. Paint each square individually. Suggested colors for each square are shown in Figure F, pages 35, 36 and 37.

3. After you finish the squares, set them aside to dry overnight.

Sewing the squares

1. Cut a matching "back" for each square from the lining fabric.

2. Pin the back and front of the square right sides together. Stitch together along the outer lines, leaving an unstitched opening large enough to turn the square right side out.

3. Clip the corners and seams, turn right side out and press gently.

4. Topstitch around all 4 edges.

5. Sew nylon fasteners (or snaps) to the front of the tote and the back of each square. Attach the squares to the front of the tote.

Figure B

Figure C

Figure D

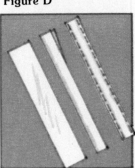

Figure E

Figure F

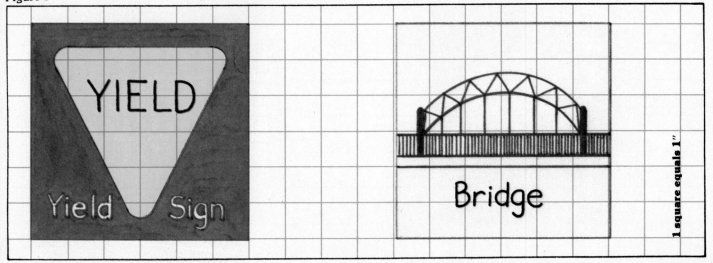

1 square equals 1"

Figure F

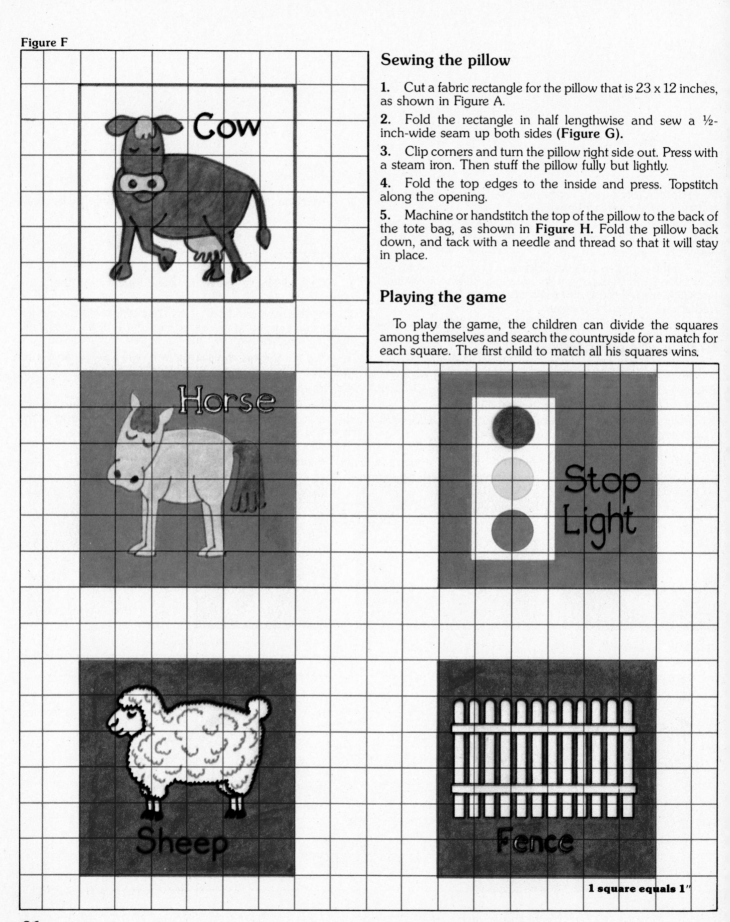

1 square equals 1″

Sewing the pillow

1. Cut a fabric rectangle for the pillow that is 23 x 12 inches, as shown in Figure A.

2. Fold the rectangle in half lengthwise and sew a ½-inch-wide seam up both sides (**Figure G**).

3. Clip corners and turn the pillow right side out. Press with a steam iron. Then stuff the pillow fully but lightly.

4. Fold the top edges to the inside and press. Topstitch along the opening.

5. Machine or handstitch the top of the pillow to the back of the tote bag, as shown in **Figure H.** Fold the pillow back down, and tack with a needle and thread so that it will stay in place.

Playing the game

To play the game, the children can divide the squares among themselves and search the countryside for a match for each square. The first child to match all his squares wins.

Figure F

Figure G

Figure H

House

Flowers

Chicken

Train

Truck

1 square equals 1″

Child's Quiet Book

A sturdy, cloth book designed to provide silent activity for young children. It's also a learning tool that teaches about helping others and encourages basic dexterity skills.

Figure A

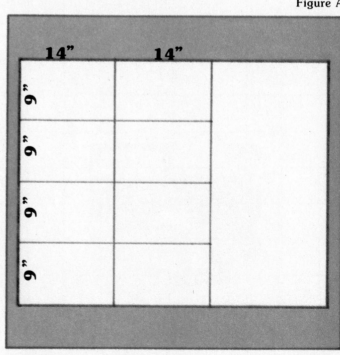

Materials

1¼ yards of medium weight white cotton fabric.
10 nylon fastener "spots".
1 short shoestring to fit a 2- or 3-eyelet shoe.
1 large button.
2 large snaps.
2 large hooks with eyelets.
Small amount of polyester fiberfill.
Masking tape.
Black waterproof marker.
Dressmaker's carbon paper, tracing paper, and soft pencil.
White sewing thread, needle, scissors, pinking shears, straight pins, and iron.
Artist's acrylic paint in the following colors: white, black, red, blue, and yellow. (With these 5 colors you can mix the rest of the colors you will need.)
Artist's paint brush in a very small size.

MY QUIET BOOK OF FOREST FRIENDS

Mr. and Mrs. Rabbit can't find the children.

Can you?
Put them in the cozy rabbit hole.

HOW MANY ANIMALS IN THE

FOREST CAN YOU HELP?

Mr. and Mrs. Bird are building a nest. Can you help them finish?

Barney Bear is going to sleep for the winter.
Please close the door.

Figure B

Mr. Fish likes leafy green plants in his pond. Can you find some?

Freddie Fox wants to cross the creek. Can you fasten the log?

Can you help Mr. Squirrel hide his acorns?

THIS BOOK WAS MADE ESPECIALLY FOR
BY

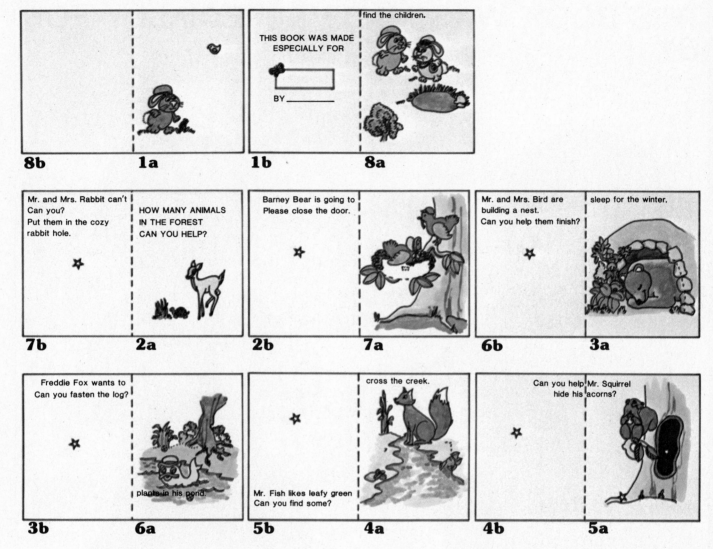

Figure C

Cutting the pieces

1. Cut 8 fabric rectangles, each 9 x 14 inches, from the white cotton fabric as shown in **Figure A.** These will be the pages of the book.

2. Transfer the full-size patterns **(Figure B, pages 39 through 49,)** onto the book pages using the carbon paper and a soft pencil. Refer to **Figure C** for pattern placement. DO NOT transfer the writing onto any pages except pages 1a, 1b, and 2a.

3. Fold the remaining portion of the cotton fabric (17 x 36 inches) in half so you have a 17 x 18-inch rectangle of double thickness. Pin the 2 thicknesses together.

4. Transfer the remaining pieces (log, green plant, den door, rabbit hole cover, right and left bird's nest, acorns, and boy's front) onto the double-thick rectangle.

5. Pin each of the individual pieces to both layers and cut out, leaving a ⅜-inch margin around each piece.

6. Transfer the boy's back onto the second thickness which you have cut to match the front. You now have a front and back for each of the extra pieces. All of the backs will be blank with the exception of the boy's.

Painting

1. Paint each of the pages and all of the extra pieces, following the colors shown on the full-size patterns. Tips on painting are given in the "Techniques" section at the front of this book. Feel free to change any of the colors if you desire.

2. Let the paint dry overnight.

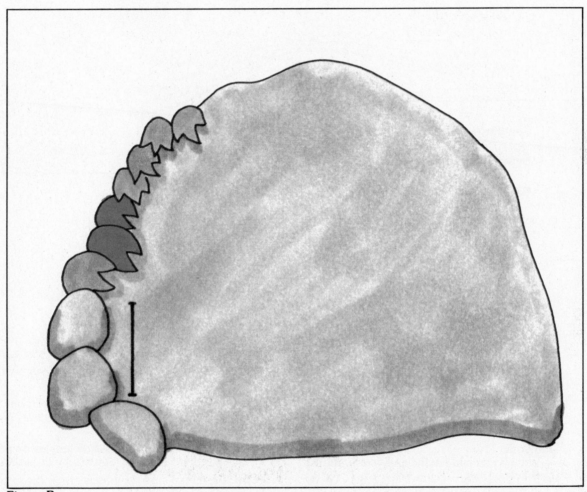

Figure B

Handwork

1. Pin each of the extra pieces right side down on top of the matching blank back. Pin the front and back together. Sew along the dotted lines, leaving an opening large enough to turn and stuff the sewn piece.

2. Clip all corners and curves, and turn the piece right side out. Stuff the piece lightly with fiberfill and whipstitch the opening closed.

3. Refer to the marking guide given in **Figure D** and to the full-size patterns for the rest of the hand finishing.

4. Extra Pieces — Handwork: Work buttonholes in both the right and left bird's nest pieces. Make 1 large buttonhole in the bear's den door. Sew 1 large snap on the back of the fish's leaves. Sew 2 large hooks on the back of the fox's log. Sew 1 nylon fastener "spot" on the back of the acorns. Sew 1 nylon fastener "spot" on the back of the little boy.

49

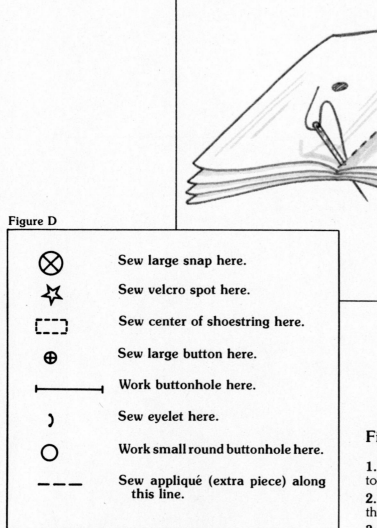

Figure D

⊗   **Sew large snap here.**

☆   **Sew velcro spot here.**

⌐ ⌐   **Sew center of shoestring here.**

⊕   **Sew large button here.**

├──────┤   **Work buttonhole here.**

)   **Sew eyelet here.**

◯   **Work small round buttonhole here.**

─ ─ ─   **Sew appliqué (extra piece) along this line.**

5.   Pages — Handwork:
 - Page 1b — Write your child's name and your name in black waterproof marker.
 - Page 8a — Sew 2 nylon fastener spots. Whipstitch the rabbit hole cover in place.
 - Page 7b — Sew nylon fastener spot.
 - Page 2b — Sew nylon fastener spot.
 - Page 7a — Whipstitch bird nest pieces (right and left) in place. Fold the shoestring in half and sew center point where indicated.
 - Page 6b — Sew nylon fastener spot.
 - Page 3a — Sew button. Whipstitch den door in place.
 - Page 3b — Sew nylon fastener spot.
 - Page 6a — Sew 2 large snaps.
 - Page 5b — Sew nylon fastener spot.
 - Page 4a — Whipstitch log in place. Sew two eyelets where indicated.
 - Page 4b — Sew nylon fastener spot.
 - Page 5a — Sew 2 nylon fastener spots.

Finishing

1.   Place first 2 rectangular pages back to back, and pin them together. Pages 1a and 1b should be back to back.

2.   Sew around all 4 sides and down the center of the double thickness. Pink the outer edges.

3.   Repeat steps 1 and 2 for the 2 rectangles (page 2a back to back with 2b), and then for the remaining rectangles (3a and 3b, 4a and 4b).

4.   Stack the 4 double-thickness rectangles on top of each other and pin them together down the center line.

5.   Check to make sure the pages are in the correct order, and the book reads right. Then sew down the center through all the thicknesses **(Figure E)**.

6.   Transfer the remaining lettering, referring to Figure C for placement. It is easier to use a marker to color the lettering rather than to use paint and brush.

The book is arranged so that the child can move the little boy through the book from page to page, attaching him on each page. The child can button the bear's den door; hook the log for the fox; put the acorns in the tree for the squirrel; move and snap the green plants to the fish pond; lace the bird's nest together; and move the rabbit babies to the rabbit hole under their cover.

We have had good luck washing our completed book in hot water. However, as a precautionary measure, we recommend using cold water on the gentle cycle.

THE FRONT BURNER
hot projects for your kitchen

Projects In This Section:

Country Morning Rooster

This cheerful rooster will greet you each day with his silent crowing. Hang him on your kitchen wall and he'll start your morning with a smile.

Materials

¾ yard of bright yellow fabric.
¾ yard of brown calico fabric.
Scraps of red/orange fabric.
½ yard of white and orange calico fabric.
¼ yard of white and brown calico fabric.
1 yard of 3-ply bonded polyester quilt batting.
1 piece of double-thickness mounting board (or thin
    plywood), 20 x 28 inches.
⅛- or ¼-inch-thick sheet of styrofoam, 28 x 20 inches (or
    substitute heavy cardboard).
Scissors, razor knife, straight pins, white glue, needle, and
    thread.
Dressmaker's carbon paper, tracing paper, and pencil.

Cutting the pieces

1. Enlarge the patterns given in **Figure A** to full size. Transfer each of the 3 enlarged body patterns (rooster body, head, and feet) onto the styrofoam sheet (or heavy cardboard), and cut out with a razor knife. Cut slowly and carefully to make the edges as smooth as possible.

2. Cover the front of each styrofoam pattern piece with a matching layer of quilt batting. Glue in place.

3. Place each pattern piece face down on the wrong side of the appropriate color of fabric (see Figure A), and trace around it. Notice that the top portion of the rooster body is covered with orange fabric, and the bottom portion is covered with brown calico. Don't worry about the raw edges where these fabrics meet, as they will be covered later by the rooster head.

4. Cut out each traced fabric piece, adding a 1½-inch fabric allowance around the outer edges.

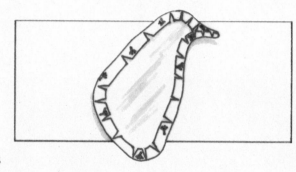

Figure B

Figure A

1 square equals 1″

5. Wipe or spray glue on the wrong side of the styrofoam. Center and place the styrofoam (batting side down) on the matching fabric piece.

6. Pull and smooth the fabric across the front and glue the edges to the back. Clip corners and curves to eliminate any excess fabric on the back of the pattern piece **(Figure B)**. Use straight pins to hold the fabric edges on the back until the glue dries.

7. Wipe a very thin layer of glue on the front side of the 20 x 28-inch background board. Cover it with the bright yellow fabric, in the same manner used on the rooster body pieces, trimming and gluing the edges to the back.

8. Wipe a generous amount of glue on the back of the rooster body, and center it on the bright yellow background. **Figure C** shows the placement of each of the pieces in sequence. Place a heavy weight on top and let dry.

9. Cut 2 comb pieces and 2 wattle pieces from a double-thickness of orange fabric, adding a ¼-inch seam allowance. Stitch the 2 comb pieces right sides together, leaving an opening large enough to turn the piece. Repeat for the 2 wattle pieces.

10. Clip seams, turn the pieces right side out and whipstitch the opening closed.

54

Figure C

11. Wipe a thin film of glue on the comb piece and place it over the covered orange fabric on top of the rooster body.

12. Glue the rooster head and feet to the body, again placing a heavy weight on top of the pieces. Let the glue dry.

13. Glue the wattle to the top of the rooster head.

14. Cut the rooster eye from a plain brown portion of one of the calico fabrics. Glue in place.

Sewing the tailfeathers

1. Double the fabric and cut a total of 6 feather pieces from 3 different calico fabrics, 2 each from the 3 feather patterns.

2. Place 2 matching fabric feather pieces right sides together and stitch around the outer edges, ¼ inch from the outer edges. Leave the pieces open and unstitched between the small circles.

3. Clip ends and curves, turn right side out and press.

4. Lightly stuff each of the sewn "feathers" with quilt batting. Whipstitch the opening closed.

5. Machine or handstitch down the center on each of the stuffed "feathers."

6. Arrange the completed feathers on the rooster. Hold them in place with straight pins until you are happy with the arrangement (refer to Figure C for suggested placement). Hand tack each of the feathers in place.

7. The completed rooster may then be framed as you would any other picture — or simply glue ribbon trim around the covered background. We hemmed 1-inch-wide calico fabric strips, mitered them at the corners, and glued them around the outer edge of the completed picture.

Quick Quilted Potholders

These quilted potholders are inexpensive and simple to sew. The finished size is big enough to protect against even the largest roasting pan.

Figure A

1 square equals 1"

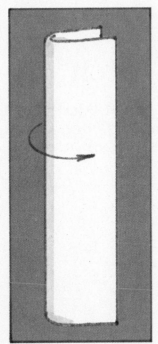

Figure B

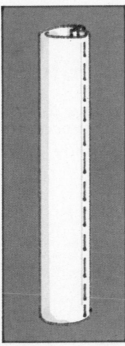

Figure C

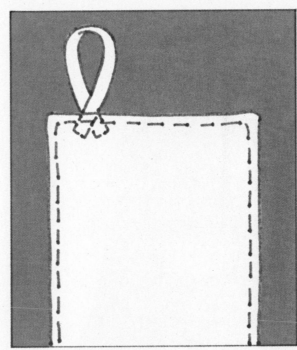

Figure D

Materials

Sturdy cotton fabric in your choice of colors. All of the potholders may be made in their individual shapes, or may be finished with a border. A total of 1½ yards of 36-inch-wide fabric is required to make all 8 individual shapes; 2½ yards if you wish to make all square or rectangular potholders. We made 4 potholders each way, and used scraps of fabric in different colors. Each potholder requires a piece of fabric slightly over twice the pattern size.

If you wish to make a two-color potholder (as in the pineapple, tomato, strawberry and salt shaker) a separate piece of fabric may be machine appliquéd over the top portion of the design.

A thin layer of quilt batting the same size as each of the potholders you make.

Paper, pencil, ruler and dressmaker's carbon paper to enlarge and transfer the patterns.

Scissors, straight pins, thread to match your fabric, iron, ironing board, sewing machine (or they can be finished by hand), and laundry markers in your choice of colors.

Transferring the patterns

1. Enlarge the patterns shown in **Figure A** to a full-size paper pattern.

2. To make the large square and rectangular bordered potholders, cut 8 squares, each 10 x 10 inches (2 each for the cabbage, artichoke, mustard jar, and tomato) and 8 rectangles, each 10 x 13 inches (for the strawberry, salt shaker, bean jar, and pineapple). For potholders without borders, cut 16 pieces, matching 2 to each pattern, and leaving a 1-inch seam allowance around the outer edges of the pattern.

3. Transfer the enlarged pattern to the center of the fabric using dressmaker's carbon paper.

4. Cut 8 pieces of quilt batting; 1 to fit each of the finished potholders.

Sewing

1. To make the hanging loops, cut 8 rectangles, each 2 inches wide and 8 inches long. Fold each rectangle in half along the 8-inch length **(Figure B)**.

2. Turn the raw edges to the inside and topstitch along the open edge, through all thicknesses **(Figure C)**.

3. Pin back and front of the potholder right sides together. Stitch around the outer edges, leaving a portion of the top edge open and unstitched where the hanging loop will be placed. Clip seams and curves and turn right side out.

4. Slip the quilt batting inside the potholder.

5. Fold one hanging loop in half and pin it inside the top of the potholder **(Figure D)**. Press.

6. Topstitch around the outside edges of the potholder. On square or rectangular potholders, topstitch around the outer edges of each individual design also.

Kitchen Witch

According to Norwegian folklore, she will keep pots from boiling over, cakes from falling, and roasts from burning.

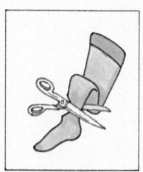

Figure A

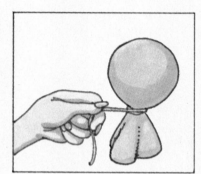

Figure B

Materials

8- or 9-inch clay flowerpot.
1½ yards dress fabric.
½ yard of contrasting apron fabric.
1 pair of baby shoes.
1 pair of baby socks.
2 nylon hose legs.
2 pounds of polyester batting.
16-inch length of ¼- or ⅜-inch-diameter wooden dowel rod.
1 package of bias tape.
Bundle of 9-inch-long straws or small twigs.
1 skein of rug yarn.
1 package of rick-rack.
Straight pins, sewing thread (to match dress, rick-rack, and bias tape), iron and ironing board, and heavy-duty sewing thread in a medium brown color.
Red and brown embroidery thread (for the facial features).
String and white glue.
Dressmaker's carbon paper, tracing paper, and pencil.

Making the head

1. Cut the foot from a nylon hose about 2 inches above the ankle.

2. Form a smooth ball of batting, about 9 inches in diameter. Compress and stuff the batting into the nylon hose foot until you have formed a round "head" about 6 inches in diameter (about 19 inches in circumference).

3. Pull part of the batting down into the "neck" portion of the hose, and tie a piece of yarn around the "neck." Tying over a portion of the batting will prevent the head from wobbling.

4. For the facial features, you will need a needle threaded with a double strand of heavy-duty sewing thread.

5. Follow the illustrations (**Figure C** through **Figure F**) to construct the facial features. Insert the threaded needle at the top of the head and bring it out on the face area on what will be the left side of the nose. Finish the bottom of the nose by bringing the thread out at an angle. Run the thread back up to the top of the head and secure.

6. To form the eyes, bring the thread through from the back of the head to the front, then to the back of the head again. Repeat on the other side.

7. To form the mouth, first make 2 "dimples" in the same manner as the eyes, only lower.

8. Connect the "dimples" using a full strand of dark red embroidery floss and the split stitch.

9. To finish the eyes, embroider the eye sockets with a full strand of brown embroidery floss using the satin stitch.

Your face will not look exactly like the one in the photograph. Even when the same person does the face twice in a row, it will vary slightly. However, that is what makes your witch individual — unlike any other.

Figure C

Figure D

Figure E

Figure F

Figure G

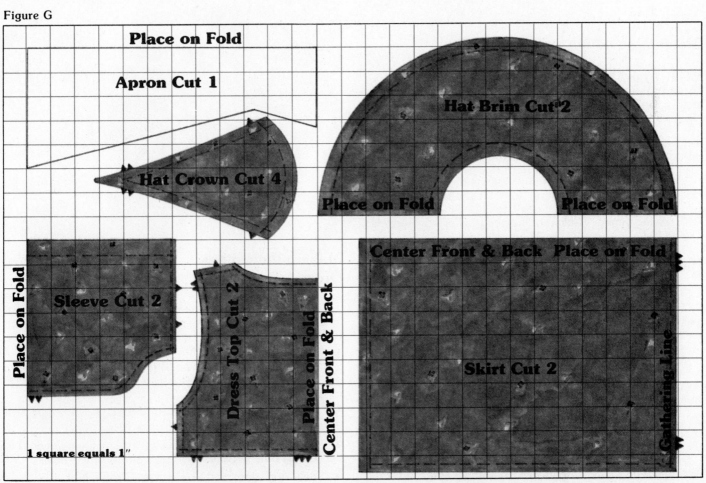

Place on Fold

Apron Cut 1

Hat Brim Cut 2

Hat Crown Cut 4

Place on Fold

Place on Fold

Place on Fold

Sleeve Cut 2

Dress Top Cut 2

Place on Fold

Center Front & Back

Center Front & Back Place on Fold

Skirt Cut 2

Gathering Line

1 square equals 1"

Figure H

Figure I

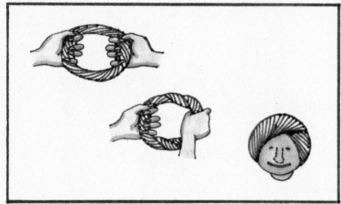

3. Slip the baby socks over the "feet," turning down the cuffs. Put the baby shoes on forcing the feet well into the shoes.

4. Cut a 20-inch length of hose from the remaining leg. This piece should include the foot part of the hose, if it is a sandal toe. (If it is a regular toe, cut the same as for the legs. Tie a piece of string tightly around one end, then turn the hose inside out so the tied knot is on the inside).

5. Stuff this 20-inch length of hose with a 30-inch length of batting, as you did for the legs, pulling the hose to the longer length.

6. Find the center of the completed "arms" and place it at the center back, forcing it between the head and the flower pot as shown in Figure K.

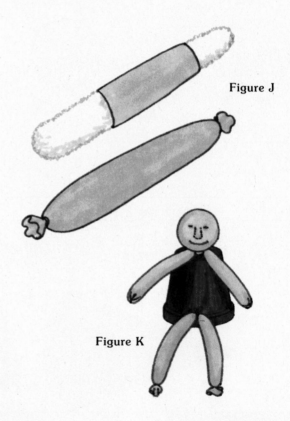

Figure J

Figure K

Making the body

1. Invert the flower pot and wrap it with a thin layer of batting. Attach the head by pulling the "neck" through the hole in the bottom of the flower pot. The neck should fit very tightly inside the hole **(Figure H)**.

2. Use a full skein of rug yarn to make the hair. Remove the label carefully and you should find that the rug yarn is coiled in a single circular roll. Hold the roll open in both hands **(Figure I)**. Grip one side of the roll in your left hand. With your right hand, twist the other side of the roll about 3 times. Set the roll on top of the witch's "head" and tack it in place with sewing thread. The top of the head will be covered later by the hat.

Making the arms and legs

1. Cut a 20-inch length of leg from the same hose from which you cut the head piece. Form a long 30-inch smooth piece of quilt batting (about 2 inches in diameter). The batting should not be terribly solid, but rather pliable. Insert the 30-inch length of batting through the 20-inch shorter length of hose **(Figure J)**. Pull the hose on both ends until it is the same length as the batting. Tie a string around each end to secure it. The string should be tied over a small portion of the batting to keep it in place. This tube will form both legs.

2. Cut a long piece of string. Tie the middle of the string securely around the middle of the leg tube. Tie a knot. Wrap the long ends of the string completely around the flower pot, using the lip of the pot as a guideline. Tie the string in a knot. This will hold the legs on the front of the pot **(Figure K)**.

Making the clothes
Dress

1. Using dressmaker's carbon paper and tracing paper, enlarge the dress patterns and transfer them to the material. Place the 2 Dress Tops right sides together and sew the shoulder seams.

2. Slit the center back about 6 inches deep **(Figure L)**. Turn the raw edges along the slit to the wrong side of the fabric to form a hem. Topstitch.

3. Gather the top of Sleeve and sew (right sides together) to open armhole, easing to fit **(Figure M)**.

4. Hem the bottom of the sleeves, turning the raw edges to the wrong side. Topstitch rick-rack around the sleeve.

5. Sew underarm and side seams **(Figure N)**.

60

Figure L   Figure M   Figure P

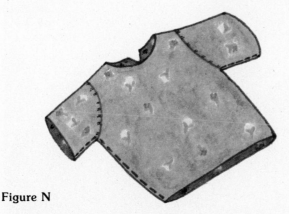

Figure N   **Figure Q**   **Figure R**

6. Sew the 2 Skirt pieces together at the side seams, right sides together.

7. Turn up the hem allowance on the skirt and stitch. Add rick-rack around the bottom of the skirt.

8. Gather the skirt along the top gathering line.

9. With right sides together, sew the skirt to the dress top, matching notches and easing gathers to fit.

10. Slip the dress onto the witch, and tack the neck opening closed in the back.

Apron

1. Encase the top of edge of Apron with bias tape, following the instructions given on the package.

2. Encase the remaining edges of the apron with bias tape. Leave a 10-inch length where you begin and end. These will be the apron ties **(Figure O)**.

Figure O

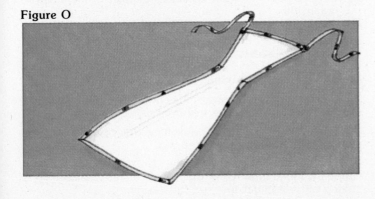

3. Tie the loose apron ends around the neck so that the apron waist is even with the dress waist.

4. Cut a length of bias tape (about 1 yard long). Place it over the apron around the waist and tie the ends in a bow in back.

Hat

1. Sew the 4 Hat Crown pieces right sides together, forming a peaked crown **(Figure P)**. Press and turn right side out.

2. Place the 2 Hat Brim pieces right sides together and stitch around the outer edges **(Figure Q)**. Clip the seam all the way around, turn right side out, and press.

3. Sew completed crown to brim **(Figure R)**. Press seam to inside of crown.

4. Stuff hat crown loosely with batting, allowing the peak to crumple at the end.

5. Place the hat on the witch and tack in place with sewing thread.

Finishing

1. To make the broomstick, tie the straws or small twigs securely around the wooden dowel rod using a piece of string. Add a small amount of white glue so that the straws will stay in place. After the glue has dried, tie a short length of bias tape around the "broomstick" to cover the string.

2. Set the finished witch on a small stool, on a box or anyplace that will elevate the body, allowing the legs to hang down. Place the broomstick in front, lapping the hand over the stick. Tack the hand in place.

Stenciled Tablecloth

Stencil this country-look tablecloth with ordinary latex enamel paint on a twin-size muslin sheet. It's surprisingly easy to transform your dining room or kitchen from ordinary to great-looking.

Materials

A small amount of good quality latex enamel paint (or artist's acrylic paints) in light green and deep red. This is a good project to use up leftover latex enamel paint if you happen to have it on hand.

A good quality small paint brush, ½- or ¾-inch wide and an artist's brush in a small size for touch-up work. Special stenciling brushes are available which are made specifically for this purpose, but ordinary paint brushes work quite well.

A sheet of fairly heavy clear plastic. Here again, special stenciling material is available for this specific purpose. However, a sheet of plastic designed to cover photos in an album serves the purpose. The heavier the plastic, the more difficult it is to cut the stencil, but the easier it is to handle the stencil while painting.

A very sharp razor knife with a pointed blade. Keep several extra blades on hand and replace them if the stencil becomes difficult to cut. Blades are not expensive and a sharp knife is a big timesaver.

You'll also need some masking tape, clean rags, a small container of water to clean your brushes, and a very hard surface on which to cut your stencil. A piece of glass is a perfect cutting surface, but it should be taped on the edges to protect your hands.

2 twin-size muslin sheets (1 for the back and 1 for the front of the tablecloth).

A thin layer of washable quilt batting to fit between the top and bottom layers of the tablecloth.

12 yards of green bias tape to bind the edges of the finished tablecloth.

Dressmaker's carbon paper, tracing paper, and pencil.

Cutting the stencil

1. Enlarge the stencil patterns shown in **Figure A** to full size.

2. Place the plastic on top of the chosen stencil pattern and tape the 2 pieces together with masking tape.

3. Place the taped pattern and stencil on top of the cutting surface, with the plastic on top.

4. Cut out each of the smaller designs first. If you wish, you can use a metal ruler to cut the straight lines. The last step is cutting out the larger areas of the design.

1 square equals 1"

Figure A

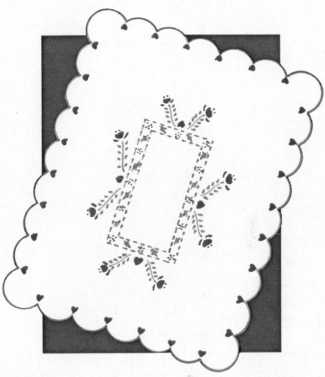

Figure B

Applying the paint

When stenciling, apply a coat of paint through the stencil holes as evenly as possible. To do this, dab just the end of a very dry brush in the paint. This will give you even coverage of the area to be stenciled, as well as eliminate drips and runs. You will probably want to practice a little before you begin working on the actual project.

Instead of cutting 2 different stencils, we applied masking tape to the back of the stencil over the holes which we did not want to show. When painting the stenciled leaves, tape over the flowers, and you will not risk getting green paint where you intended to have red paint. If you do get out of the lines, you can touch up with a small artist's brush after the stencil has dried.

1. Center a rectangle of the Border Stencil in the middle of a twin sheet. The rectangle will have an outer dimension of approximately 21 x 37½ inches **(Figure B)**.

2. Center the heart of the Heart Stencil on each of the 4 sides of the center rectangle, and stencil.

3. Wash the Heart Stencil, flip it over, and stencil again for the remaining side of the design (the heart in the pattern will align with the previously stenciled heart).

Sewing

1. Place the unpainted remaining twin sheet on your flat work surface. Make sure it is straight and smooth. Lay the matching size quilt batting over it. Lay the stenciled twin sheet on top of the batting, right side up.

2. Pin the 3 layers together securely. Begin pinning in the center and work out to the 4 sides, smoothing the layers as you pin.

3. It will make your sewing and handling of the 3 layers easier if you baste them together at this point. Begin basting in the center and work out to the edges.

4. Using matching thread, machine stitch the outside edges of the borders, flowers, hearts, and leaves. Keep the work flat as you stitch.

5. Use the Scallop Pattern to cut scallops around all 4 outer edges of the tablecloth.

6. Pin all 3 layers together around the scallops and stitch along the outer edge about ¼ inch from the scallops.

7. Encase the raw edges in bias tape.

8. Using the Heart Stencil, paint a heart only at the top of each of the scallops.

63

Autumn Leaves Clock

This easy-to-make clock will add a decorator touch to your kitchen. Cut, stuff and sew the leaves and attach them to a plywood or cardboard box base. The clockworks can be purchased or recycled from an old kitchen clock.

Materials

20-inch square of bright yellow fabric to cover the clock base.

A plywood or heavy cardboard box, 14 inches square and 2¾ inches deep.

Clockworks with hands not more than 3½ inches long. Buy a battery-operated clockwork or disassemble an old electric clock.

Fabric scraps for the leaves. One leaf requires 2 fabric rectangles, each 6 x 7½ inches. There are 16 leaves, so you will need 32 squares. We used 4 different colors: deep red, brown, white, and dusty rose.

A small amount of polyester quilt batting.

Sewing machine, scissors, and straight pins.

White glue.

Tracing paper and pencil.

Making the leaves

1. A full-size leaf pattern is given in **Figure A.** Trace the pattern and use it to cut 16 matching leaf fronts and backs from cotton fabric. The leaf back pattern is the reverse of the leaf front.

2. Place a matching leaf front and back right sides together and stitch a ¼-inch seam, leaving an opening between the 2 small circles to allow for turning and stuffing.

3. Clip the seam allowance and turn the leaf right side out. Press gently with a steam iron.

4. Stuff the leaf lightly with polyester batting and whipstitch the opening closed, turning the raw edges to the inside.

5. Machine stitch a vein pattern on each leaf, stitching through all layers **(Figure B).**

6. Repeat steps 2 through 5 for the remaining 15 leaves.

Figure A

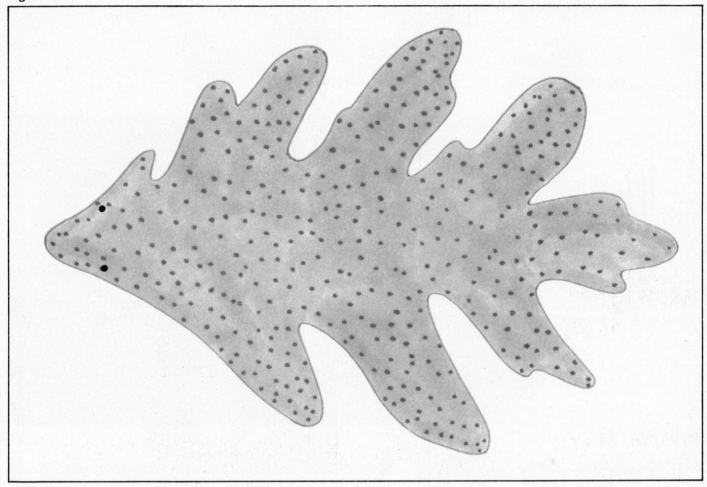

Making the clock base

1. Cut a hole in the center front of the plywood or cardboard clock base large enough to accommodate the clock mechanism.

2. Place the 20-inch-square yellow fabric right side down on a work surface.

3. Wipe a generous amount of white glue over the front, sides, and on the inner sides of the clock base. Center the base (glued side down) on the fabric square.

4. Smooth and stretch the fabric across the clock front. Pull the fabric up and over the sides and glue it to the inner sides. Hold the fabric in place with straight pins or thumbtacks until the glue dries.

Finishing

1. Lay the fabric-covered base right side up on your work surface and place the 16 leaves on top of the clock. Move the leaves around until you have the arrangement you wish (refer to the photograph for suggested placement). Make sure that you allow enough room in the center of the clock so that the clock hands can move freely.

Figure B

2. Permanently glue the leaves in place. If you have used a plywood base, you can add tiny nails through the leaf into the base. For cardboard, use straight pins if you wish. Make sure that the pins and nails are not visible when you finish.

3. Follow the instructions on the package for installing the clockwork and attaching the hands.

Canister Cover-ups

Turn empty coffee cans into designer originals with fabric covers. Each cover-up has a clever kitchen design to label its contents.

Figure A

Small Top

Loop

Large Top

Place on Fold

Center Front

Bottom Hem

Small Side

Top Seam

Place on Fold

Center Front

Bottom Hem

Large Side

Top Seam

1 square equals 1"

Materials

1 yard of 36-inch-wide heavy cotton fabric (or stiffen a lighter
　　fabric with the addition of an interlining material).
A black laundry marker (or any color you prefer).
The canister covers are made to fit standard 1- and 2-pound
　　coffee cans. You will need 2 cans each size to use as
　　containers under the canister covers. Most coffee cans
　　now come with reuseable plastic lids.
To transfer the full-size canister designs, you will need tracing
　　paper, a soft pencil and dressmaker's carbon paper.
Iron, ironing board, sewing machine, and thread to match the
　　fabric you have chosen.

Cutting the pieces

1. Enlarge the patterns given in **Figure A** to full size.

2. Cut 2 each of the Large Top, Small Top, Large Side,
Small Side, and 4 of the Loop pattern. Pay particular attention to the "place on fold" notations on the pattern pieces.

3. The transfer designs for the front of the canister covers
are given in **Figure B.** Enlarge the patterns and transfer them
to the center of each canister side piece using dressmaker's
carbon paper. The "Flour" and "Sugar" designs fit on the
Large Side pieces, and the "Coffee" and "Tea" designs fit on
the Small Side pieces **(Figure C).** Paint with laundry marker.

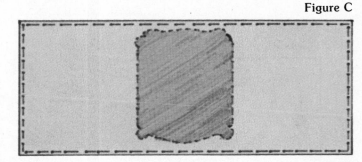

Figure C

Figure B

1 square equals 1″

67

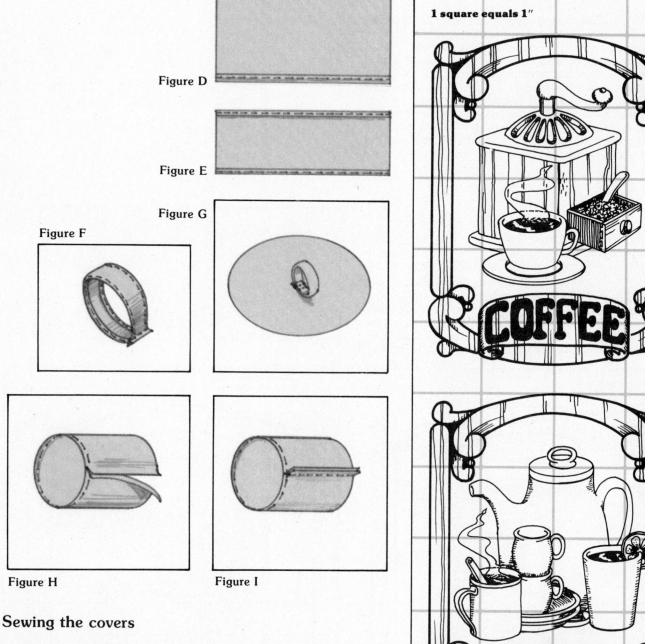

Figure D

Figure E

Figure G

Figure F

Figure H

Figure I

1 square equals 1"

COFFEE

TEA

Figure B

Sewing the covers

1. Turn the bottom hem of the side pieces to the wrong side of the fabric and machine or hand stitch in place as shown in **Figure D.**

2. Turn the hem allowances on the loop pieces to the inside and topstitch in place (**Figure E**). Sew the 2 ends together as shown in **Figure F.**

3. Open the loop and pin the sewn seam to the center of one Top, with the seam against the Top. Machine stitch in place using double stitching (**Figure G**).

4. Pin the Large Top to 1 Large Side with right sides together, leaving the seam free as shown in **Figure H.** Machine stitch.

5. Pin the back seam allowances together as shown in **Figure I** and machine stitch in place.

6. Turn the completed canister cover right side out and press gently with an iron.

7. Repeat steps 1 through 6 for the remaining 3 canister covers. If a permanent laundry marker has been used, the covers can be washed on a gentle cycle when necessary.

68

THE CHRISTMAS STOCKING
decorations for  Yuletide

Projects In This Section:

Christmas Angel

This plump little angel will top your Christmas tree, decorate a holiday table, or sit on your fireplace mantel. Or combine her with live greenery for a darling door decoration.

Materials

Scraps of calico fabric: white for the body, red for the wings, yellow for the halo, and blue for the feet.
Brown yarn for the hair.
Nylon hose.
Small amount of polyester batting for stuffing.
Needle and sewing thread.
Steam iron and ironing board.
Straight pins, scissors, and a sewing machine (or the angel can be made by hand).
Red and brown embroidery thread.
Dressmaker's carbon paper, tracing paper, and pencil.

Making the body

1. Enlarge the pattern pieces given in **Figure A** to full size.

2. Cut 1 body and 2 arm pieces from white calico fabric. Cut 4 foot pieces from blue calico fabric.

3. With right sides together, sew the arm side seams as shown in **Figure B,** and turn the arm right side out.

4. Gather one end of the arm piece ¼ inch from the raw edge.

5. Repeat steps 3 and 4 for the remaining arm piece.

6. Lay one body piece on a flat surface, right side up as shown in **Figure C.** Place arm pieces on top of body piece, matching notches.

7. Place remaining body piece right side down on top of arm and body pieces. Pin in place. Sew down both side seams through body piece and arms.

8. Turn body right side out and gather along bottom and top ¼ inch from the raw edge **(Figure D).**

9. Pull the bottom gathers and secure by stitching the opening together, turning all raw edges to the inside.

10. Stuff the body lightly but firmly and pull the top gathers together. Stitch the top of the body closed, turning the raw edges to the inside.

11. Stuff the arms lightly. Pull the gathers on the ends of the arms. Tuck the raw edges inside and stitch to secure **(Figure E).**

12. To make the feet, stitch 2 foot pieces right sides together, leaving an opening between the 2 small circles **(Figure F).** Clip the seams, turn right side out, and press.

13. Stuff the feet, turn the raw edges on the opening to the inside, and whipstitch the opening closed.

14. Whipstitch the completed feet to the bottom of the completed body.

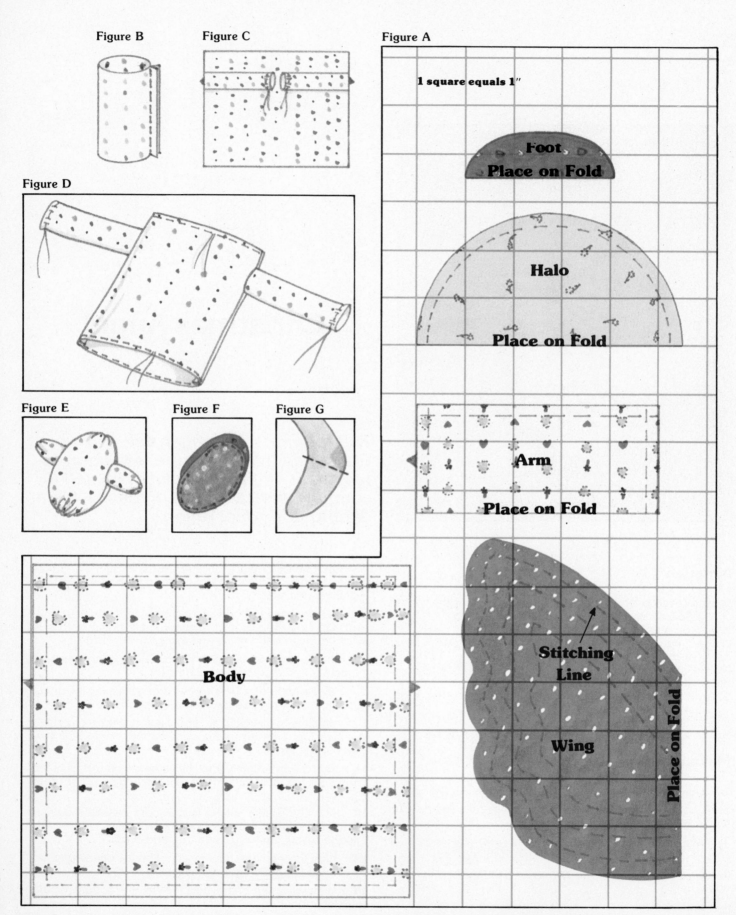

Figure B

Figure C

Figure A

1 square equals 1"

Foot
Place on Fold

Halo

Place on Fold

Figure D

Arm

Place on Fold

Figure E

Figure F

Figure G

Stitching
Line

Body

Wing

Place on Fold

72

Figure H

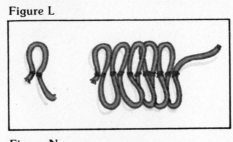

Figure I

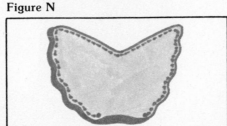

Figure J

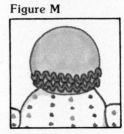

Figure K

Figure L

Figure M

Figure N

Figure O

Figure P

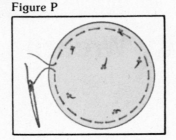

Figure Q

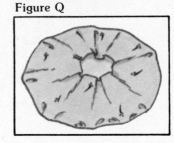

Making the head and hands

1. Cut a portion of the foot from a nylon hose **(Figure G)**.

2. Form a smooth ball of polyester batting about 5 inches in diameter. Pull the nylon hose over the batting and compress the batting until you have a round "head" about 3 inches in diameter **(Figure H)**. Tie sewing thread around the bottom of the head to secure it.

3. To form the nose, pinch up a ball in the middle of the face and wrap it tightly several times with light brown thread **(Figure I)**.

4. Embroider the features with a double strand of embroidery thread and the split stitch **(Figure J)**. Illustrated instructions for embroidery stitches are given in the "Tips and Techniques" section at the front of this book. Use brown thread for the eyes and red thread for the mouth.

5. Sew the completed head to the body as shown in **Figure K**.

6. To form the hands, cut 2 pieces of nylon hose and wrap them around a piece of batting slightly larger than a cotton ball.

7. Tie the hands at the bottom with thread in the same manner as the head, and sew them to the ends of the arms.

8. Bring the arms together in front, and sew the hands together as shown in the photograph.

9. To make the angel's hair **(Figure L)**, begin by tacking the end of the yarn at the back of the neck. Make a loop about ½ inch long and tack again. Tack another loop in the opposite direction. Continue looping in alternate directions, working in a circle around the head, until the entire head is covered **(Figure M)**.

Sewing the wings

1. Cut 2 wing pieces from red calico fabric.

2. Place the wing pieces right sides together and sew around the outer edges, leaving them unstitched between the 2 small circles **(Figure N)**. Clip the seams, turn the wings right side out and press gently.

3. Cut a layer of batting slightly smaller than the wings, and insert it inside the wings, making sure that it is flat and evenly distributed.

4. Whipstitch the opening at the bottom of the wings closed.

5. Quilt along the 2 pattern quilting lines by either hand or machine, stitching through all 3 layers **(Figure O)**. Hand tack the center of the wings to the back of the angel's body.

6. Cut 1 halo piece from yellow calico fabric.

7. Gather the outer edges of the halo ¼ inch from the outer edge **(Figure P)**.

8. Pull gathers together and press the resulting halo flat **(Figure Q)**. Hand tack the halo on the angel's head, placing the gathers on the underside.

Fabric Holly Wreath

An "evergreen" holly wreath to stitch and stuff for your door.

Materials

½ yard red print fabric for bow and berries.

⅔ yard fabric, white with green polka dots (or any light green fabric).

1½ yards fabric, green with white polka dots (or any bright green fabric).

14-inch styrofoam wreath base (or a coathanger bent into a circle and plumped out with batting or rags).

½ pound of polyester quilt batting.

Scissors, thread, needle, and straight pins.

Dressmaker's carbon paper, tracing paper, and pencil.

Making the wreath

1. Cover the wreath base with the bright green fabric, piecing the fabric together if necessary. It will require a piece of fabric approximately 48 x 10 inches, depending on the thickness of the base. Overlap and whipstitch the fabric together on the back of the wreath base.

2. Enlarge the patterns shown in **Figure A.** Transfer the holly leaf pattern onto a doubled thickness of bright green fabric and cut 24 holly leaves (12 fronts and 12 backs).

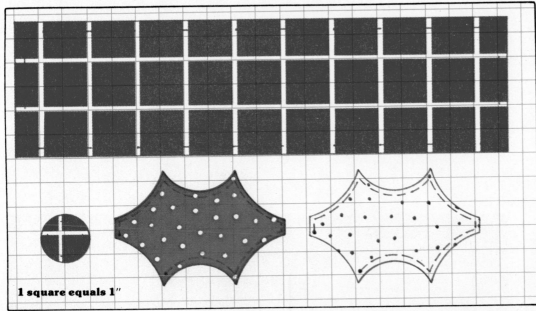

1 square equals 1"

Figure A

Figure B

Figure C

Figure D

Figure E

3. Cut 24 more holly leaves, this time using the light green fabric.

4. With right sides together, stitch 2 holly leaves of the same fabric along the dotted lines, leaving them open between small circles, as shown in **Figure B.**

5. Clip the curves and trim the angles; turn leaf right side out and press. Stuff lightly and whipstitch opening closed.

6. Repeat steps 4 and 5 for remaining 23 leaves.

7. Double the red print fabric and cut out 6 berry patterns, forming 12 circles. Stuff and gather each of the 12 circles along the dotted lines, as shown in **Figure C.**

8. Cut 2 bow patterns from the red fabric and stitch them together to form 1 long continuous strip, as shown in **Figure D.** Fold the long strip in half along the length. Sew along the raw edges, leaving 1 end open. Turn right side out, press and whipstitch the end closed.

9. Tie the red fabric bow as shown in **Figure E.**

10. Arrange the completed leaves and berries around the wreath as shown in the photograph. Hand tack them securely in place. Sew the completed bow at the bottom of the wreath.

Handmade Christmas Ornaments

Perky Christmas ornaments will brighten up your home this year. Hang them on your tree, decorate packages or wreaths, or give them as special Christmas gifts. They also make terrific sellers at a bazaar.

Materials

1 yard of white cotton fabric (or muslin).
Artist's acrylic paints in 5 basic colors: red, blue, yellow, black, and white.
Artist's small paint brush.
Short lengths of yarn or string to hang the finished ornaments.
Dressmaker's carbon paper, tracing paper, pencil, and iron.

Cutting the pieces

1.   Enlarge the patterns given in **Figure A** to full size.

2.   Transfer each of the designs to the white cotton fabric, leaving 1 inch between figures.

3.   Cut out figures, leaving a ½-inch seam allowance around each one.

1 square equals 1"

Painting and sewing

1. Follow the pattern lines to paint each of the figures, using the suggested colors in Figure A. Tips on painting are given in the "Techniques" section at the front of this book.

2. After you have finished, let the ornaments dry overnight.

3. Cut a matching piece of fabric for each of the ornaments from the white cotton fabric.

4. With right sides together, pin each of the painted ornament fronts to the matching back **(Figure B).**

5. Stitch around the outer edges, leaving an opening at the top large enough to turn and stuff the figure.

6. Clip seams and turn the figure right side out. Stuff.

7. Cut a 6-inch length of yarn. Form a hanging loop and insert the 2 loop ends inside the top opening, as shown in **Figure C.**

8. Whipstitch the opening closed, securing the loop inside.

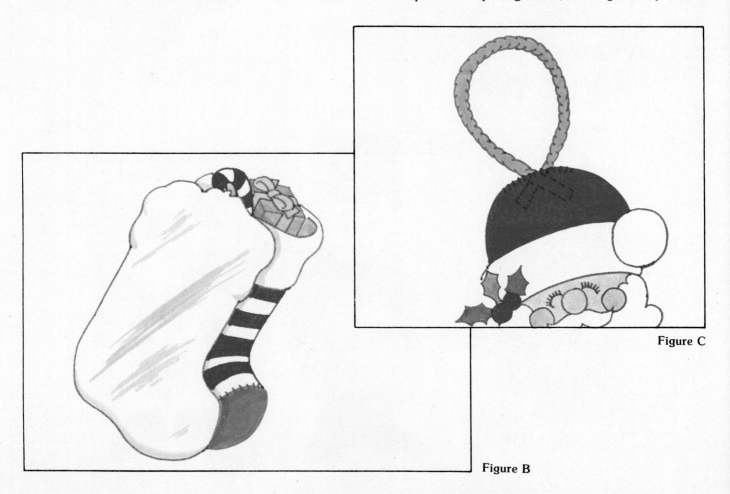

Figure C

Figure B

78

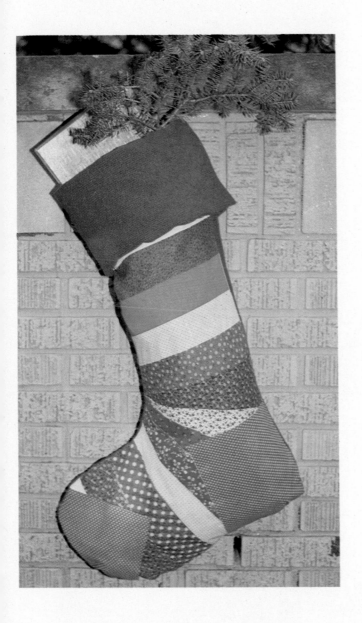

Great Big Christmas Stocking

If you're expecting Santa to bring lots of presents this year, stitch a giant Christmas stocking to hang on your front door or mantel.

Materials

14 fabric scraps, each 4 x 15 inches for the stocking stripes, in red, green, and white.
½ yard of red fabric for the stocking top.
2 pieces of red fabric for the stocking heel and toe, each 9 inches square.
1 piece of red fabric for the back of the stocking, 29 x 20 inches.
1½ yards of plain white (or solid color) fabric for the stocking front and lining.
Layer of polyester batting 24 x 7 inches.
10-inch length of wide ribbon or cording to make the hanging loop.
Sewing thread and sewing machine.
Scissors and straight pins.
Iron and ironing board.
Dressmaker's carbon paper, tracing paper, and pencil.

Sewing the stocking front

1.   Enlarge the stocking pattern given in **Figure A** to full size.

2.   Cut 1 stocking front from the lining fabric using the enlarged pattern, adding a ½-inch seam allowance on all sides.

3.   The stocking stripes are added 1 at a time, using the 4 x 15 inch fabric strips. It will look better if you alternate colors; first red, then green, and then white. Fold the raw edge under on the 15-inch side of 1 fabric strip, and press in place.

5. Pin the 2 lining pieces right sides together and stitch, leaving the top open. Do not turn right side out.

6. Slip the lining pieces inside the stocking, pin the top edges of the lining and stocking together, and stitch securely.

4. Pin the pressed fabric strip to the top edge of the stocking front **(Figure B)**.

5. Topstitch across the pressed edge of the fabric strip.

6. Fold and press a second fabric strip and pin the pressed edge over the bottom of the first strip. Topstitch the second strip in place.

7. Continue to add fabric strips to the stocking front in the same manner as for the first 2 strips. Add the strips at an angle to turn the corner at the heel **(Figure C)**. The strips do not have to cover the entire heel and toe. The 9-inch square will cover those portions.

8. Fold and press 2 adjoining edges of the 9-inch square heel and toe pieces and pin them to the stocking front **(Figure D)**.

9. Topstitch the heel and toe pieces in place.

Sewing the back and lining

1. Cut a matching back piece from red fabric.

2. Pin the stocking front and back right sides together and stitch around the sides and bottom leaving the top open.

3. Clip curves, turn right side out and press.

4. Cut 2 lining pieces, again using the enlarged stocking pattern.

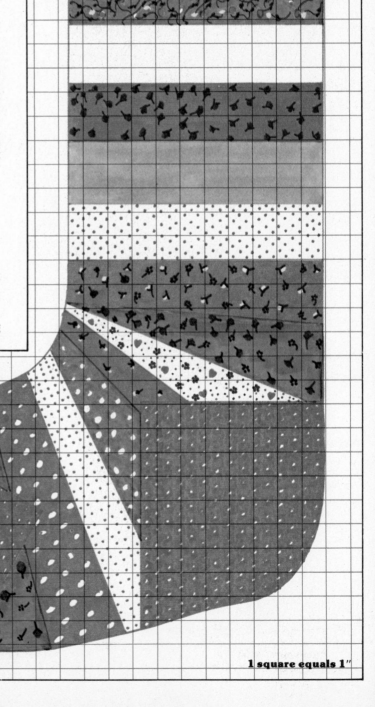

Figure A

1 square equals 1"

80

Figure B

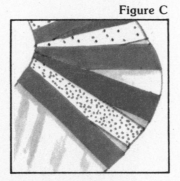

Figure C

Figure D

Figure E

Figure F

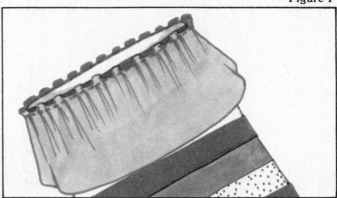

Figure G

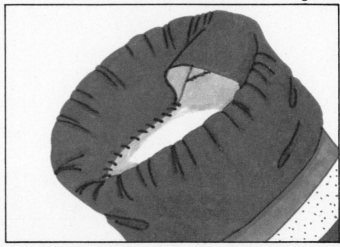

Adding the stocking top

1.   Cut a stocking top from red fabric 18 x 25 inches.

2.   Pin the two 18-inch edges right sides together and sew a ½-inch-wide seam **(Figure E)**. This seam will be the center back.

3.   Gather the stocking top and slip it (wrong side out) over the stocking, positioning the sewn seam at the center back.

4.   Pin the gathered edge to the top of the stocking, easing the gathers to fit **(Figure F)**. Sew a ½-inch seam around the top.

5.   Pin the 7 x 24-inch piece of batting to the wrong side of the stocking top, slightly above the gathering line. Baste in place, sewing through the seam allowance in both the stocking top and body.

6.   Fold the pressed edge of the top up and over the batting and pin it to the inside of the stocking **(Figure G)**. It should just cover the stitching inside the top of the stocking body. Whipstitch the pressed edge in place.

7.   Stitch a ribbon or cord loop inside the completed stocking at the side seam to hang the finished stocking.

Calico Christmas Tree

You can stitch up this perky calico Christmas tree using leftovers straight from your sewing box. The tree is sewn from fabric remnants, stuffed with quilt batting, and trimmed with odd buttons and packaged braid trim.

Figure A

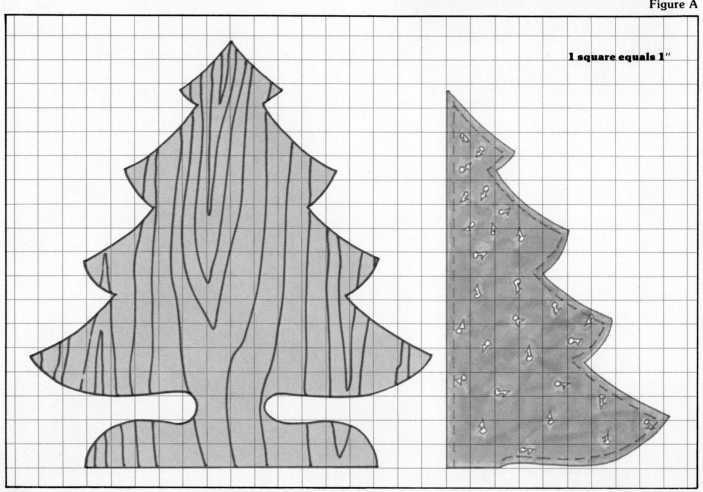

1 square equals 1"

Materials

2 pieces of ¼-inch-thick plywood, each 18 inches square.
2 yards of heavy cotton fabric in a bright green, or 8 different
    fabric pieces, each 10 x 20 inches.
2 pounds of polyester batting.
6 yards of packaged braid (or rick-rack) in a bright yellow.
Lots of odd buttons in bright colors — the more, the better.
Sewing needle and thread.
Scissors, straight pins, and white glue.
Iron and ironing board.
Dressmaker's carbon paper, tracing paper, and pencil.

Making the inner support

1. Enlarge the patterns given in **Figure A** to full size.

2. Transfer the enlarged pattern to the ¼-inch-thick
plywood and cut 2 identical inner support pieces.

3. Cut a ¼-inch-wide vertical slot in 1 plywood inner support, cutting from the top of the tree shape down to the center.
Cut a corresponding ¼-inch-wide slot in the other inner
support, cutting this one from the bottom up to the center
(Figure B). The 2 supports will then interlock to form a sturdy
inner support for your tree.

Making the fabric cover

1. The outer fabric covering is made by sewing together 8
identical fabric pieces. The pattern for the fabric covering is
given in Figure A. Cut all of the pieces from the same fabric or
combine 8 different fabrics for a patchwork look.

2. Sew 2 fabric pieces right sides together, stitching a
¼-inch-wide seam around the branch side **(Figure C).** Leave
the straight side and the bottom edge of the fabric pieces open
and unstitched.

Figure C

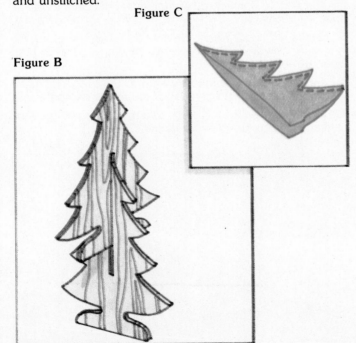

Figure B

Figure D

3. Stitch the remaining 6 fabric pieces together in sets of 2,
in the same manner as the first 2 pieces.

4. Clip curves and corners on each set, turn right side out,
and press gently.

5. Join the 4 sets right sides together along the inner straight
sides, stitching a ¼-inch-wide seam to form the fabric cover
(Figure D). Again, leave the bottom edge open and unstitched.

Finishing

1. Pad the plywood inner support with batting, gluing a
thick layer on all surfaces. Let the glue dry overnight.

2. Slip the fabric cover over the padded inner support.

3. Add batting inside the fabric covering as necessary to
plump it out.

4. Whipstitch the bottom of the fabric covering together
under each of the "branches," turning the raw edges to the
inside.

5. Sew bright buttons in a random pattern on each of the
tree branches.

6. Tack one end of the bright yellow braid at the top of the
decorated tree. Wrap the braid around the tree as you would
tinsel around a Christmas tree. Hand tack the braid to the top
of each of the branches. If it is necessary to piece the braid,
begin and end it on a branch so that it will hang evenly
between the branches.

7. Wrap several loops of braid around your fingers to form
the decoration for the top of the tree. Hand tack the loops in
place, making sure that the cut ends of the braid are not visible
on the finished tree.

Holiday Tablecloth

Create a festive Christmas touch for your holiday table with this patchwork tablecloth. Piece it together with a simple time-saving stitching technique.

Materials

The finished size of this tablecloth is 54 x 70 inches. The design and materials may be altered to fit any size table.

2 yards bright red fabric, 45 inches wide.

2 yards bright green fabric, 45 inches wide.

Layer of quilt batting 54 x 70 inches.

Full-size sheet (54 x 75 inches) for the tablecloth backing. A quilt back 54 x 70 inches or larger may be substituted.

Yardstick and tailor's chalk (or a soft pencil).

Sewing thread, sewing machine, scissors, and straight pins.

Iron and ironing board.

Cutting the pieces

This project is easy to do, but does require care in both the cutting and sewing to make sure that the patchwork blocks will match exactly on the finished tablecloth.

1. Cut 6 strips each of red and green fabric. Each of the 12 strips will measure 7 inches wide and 62½ inches long.

2. Sew 1 red and 1 green strip right sides together along the long side. Sew a ½-inch seam, as straight as possible, and press the seam open.

3. Sew a second green fabric strip to the long unstitched side of the red strip (**Figure A**). Press the seam open.

4. Continue sewing the strips together, alternating colors until all 12 strips are joined together.

Figure A

Figure B

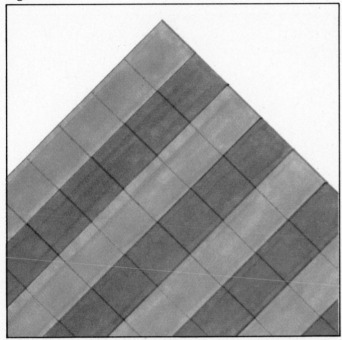

5. Working carefully with a yardstick, mark 13 lines down the sewn strips, 5 inches apart, as shown in **Figure B.**

6. Cut carefully along the marked lines down the length of the fabric strips. Leave the cut strips in their original position after they are cut.

7. Pick up the first long strip and switch it end-for-end so that a green rectangle is next to a red one **(Figure C).** Continue switching every other strip to form a patchwork pattern.

8. Place the first 2 strips right sides together and stitch along the entire length of the strips.

9. Continue to sew the remaining strips together, working in sequence. This will complete the top of the tablecloth.

Finishing

1. Place the full-size sheet on a flat work surface. Make sure it is straight and smooth. Lay the matching size quilt batting over it, then lay the patchwork tablecloth top over the batting, right side up.

2. Pin the 3 layers together securely. Begin pinning in the center and work out to the 4 sides, smoothing the layers as you pin.

3. It will make your sewing and handling of the 3 layers easier if you baste them together at this point. Baste, again beginning in the center and working out to the edges.

4. Topstitch on both sides of each of the sewn patchwork seams, about ¼ inch from the seam line. Keep the stitching as straight and even as possible **(Figure D).**

5. Trim the edges of the tablecloth backing and the batting even with the edges of the top.

6. To finish, machine stitch a 1-inch-wide hem on all 4 sides, and gently press the completed tablecloth with a steam iron.

Figure C

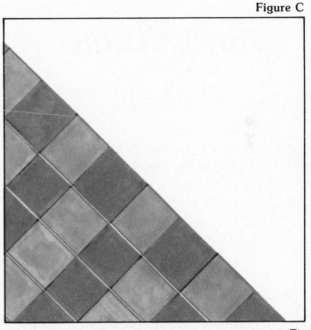

Figure D

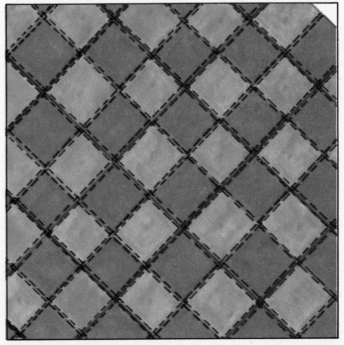

85

Tiny Tim Doll

Bring a wee bit of Olde England to your Christmas hearth this year. All you need are some fabric scraps in Christmas colors and a minimum amount of time. He'll be a favorite part of many Christmases to come.

Materials

¾ yard of white (or flesh colored) cotton fabric for the doll body.
½ yard of green polka dot fabric for the coat and hat.
½ yard of red polka dot fabric for the pants and shoes.
¼ yard of white polka dot fabric for the shirt.
Top ribbed portion cut from an old sock.
Polyester batting or other stuffing material.
Red and brown fabric paint and a small brush (or permanent markers).
Forked tree branch for Tiny Tim's crutch, a rectangular piece of cardboard, and a black marking pen.
1 skein of medium-weight yellow yarn and a needle large enough to accommodate 1 strand of yarn.
Straight pins, sewing needle, and thread to match the fabrics.
Scissors, iron, and ironing board.
Dressmaker's carbon paper, tracing paper, and pencil.

Cutting the pattern

1. Enlarge the patterns given in **Figure A** to full size.

2. Pin each full-size pattern to the appropriate color and cut out. Pay particular attention to the "place on fold" notations, and be sure to cut the number of pieces specified on each pattern.

Sewing the body

1. Place the 2 Body pieces right sides together, and sew a ½-inch seam, leaving an opening at the top of the head and the bottom of both legs (**Figure B**).

2. Clip curves, turn the body right side out, press, and stuff the body gently but fully.

3. Sew 2 Shoe pieces right sides together leaving the top open and unstitched. Turn the top seam allowance to the inside and stuff the shoe firmly.

4. Cut the ribbed portion of an old sock in half lengthwise. Fold one half wrong sides together, and sew a narrow seam up the side. Slip the socks over the bottom of the legs, slip the shoes over the bottom of the socks, and whipstitch them in place (**Figure C**).

5. Machine stitch through the arm and leg joints where indicated on the pattern pieces, sewing through all layers.

6. Paint the facial features with artist's acrylic paint using a small brush. Follow the colors given in the pattern guide. Instructions for fabric painting are given in the "Tips and Techniques" section at the beginning of this book.

7. Attach the hair along the dashes marked on the head pattern and across the back of the head. Thread the needle with an 8-inch length of yarn. Pull the yarn through the fabric and tie. Finish by cutting the yarn to different lengths.

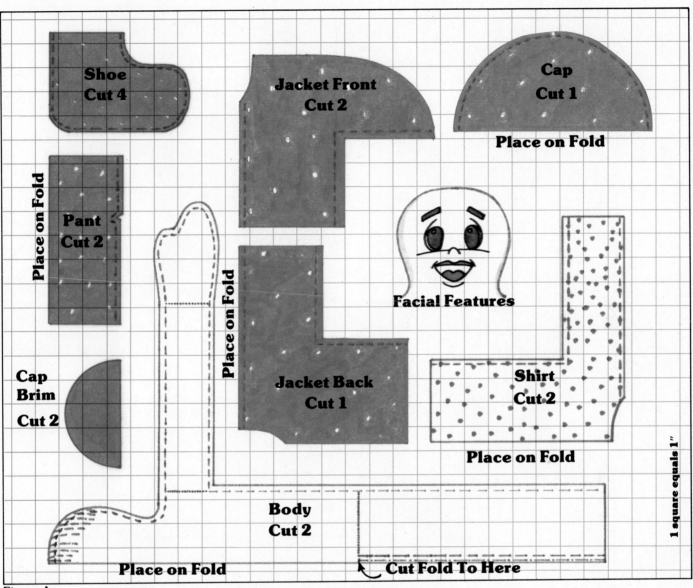

Shoe
Cut 4

Jacket Front
Cut 2

Cap
Cut 1

Place on Fold

Place on Fold

Pant
Cut 2

Place on Fold

Facial Features

Shirt
Cut 2

Cap
Brim
Cut 2

Jacket Back
Cut 1

Place on Fold

1 square equals 1"

Body
Cut 2

Place on Fold

Cut Fold To Here

Figure A

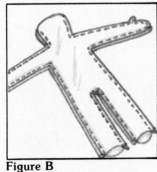

Figure B

Figure C

Figure D

Figure E

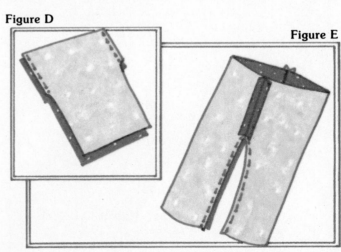

Sewing the clothes

1. Place 2 Pants pieces right sides together and sew the center front and center back seams **(Figure D)**. Refold the stitched pants, matching center front and center back seams. Sew the center leg seam **(Figure E)**.

Figure F

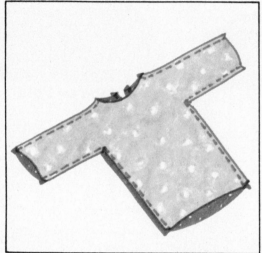

Figure G

Figure H

Figure I

2. Turn over a ½-inch seam allowance on the pant waist and at the bottom of the legs. Hem and press.

3. Pin the 2 Shirt pieces right sides together and sew the shoulder, arm and side seams. Slit the center back 2 inches deep and hem the resulting raw edges **(Figure F)**.

4. Hem the raw edges on the shirt neckline and sleeves.

5. Pin the 2 Jacket Front pieces to the Jacket Back pieces and sew the shoulder, arm, and side seams **(Figure G)**.

6. Encase the raw edges on the sleeves, neckline, jacket front, and jacket bottom with bias tape **(Figure H)**.

Finishing

1. Cut a Muffler from red fabric, 4 x 34 inches. Ravel a ¼-inch width on all 4 edges.

2. Stitch the 2 Cap Brim pieces right sides together, leaving the inside curve open and unstitched. Clip seams, turn the brim right side out, and press.

3. Gather the Cap along the stitching lines indicated on the pattern. Pull the cap-gathering threads and tie them together. Whipstitch the gathered top to the Cap Brim as shown in **Figure I,** adjusting the gathers evenly. Add a small amount of batting inside the cap.

4. Fold the cardboard rectangle in half and write "God bless us every one" on the front using a marking pen.

5. Dress the doll, beginning with the shirt. Hand tack the pants to the shirt, folding and sewing 2 pleats in the front of the pants and 2 pleats in the back so that they fit at the waist. Slip the jacket over the shirt and wrap the muffler around the neck. Hand tack the cap to the top of the head. Place the wood crutch at the side of the doll, and glue the cardboard to one hand.

THE DECORATOR TOUCH
accents for your home

Projects In This Section:

Sunshine Patchwork Bedspread

If you love the look of patchwork, but don't have six months to devote to piecing and quilting, this project is for you. It's all done on the sewing machine, so you can whip up a king-size bedspread in the time it normally takes to make a couple of patchwork pillows by hand.

Materials

This is a terrific project to use up fabric remnants you have on hand, or those that you find on sale. When choosing fabric for the project, certain basic rules should be observed:

1. All of the fabric should be of the same approximate weight. Mixing a heavy fabric with a lightweight fabric may result in a finished bedspread that will pull out of shape or have an uneven look.

2. To give the most effective look, use 3 different tones of fabric: light, medium, and dark in the same range of colors. You can mix more than 3 different fabrics, but should keep ⅓ of them light-colored, ⅓ medium, and ⅓ dark.

3. **Figure A** is drawn to show suggested colors for each of the patchwork strips. You can patch individual strips if you wish.

The bedspread also has a center panel which measures 32 inches square when finished. For that you will need 2 yards of white fabric in the same weight as the rest of the fabric you have chosen. Choose a natural fiber fabric with no nap, as it will be easier to paint on.

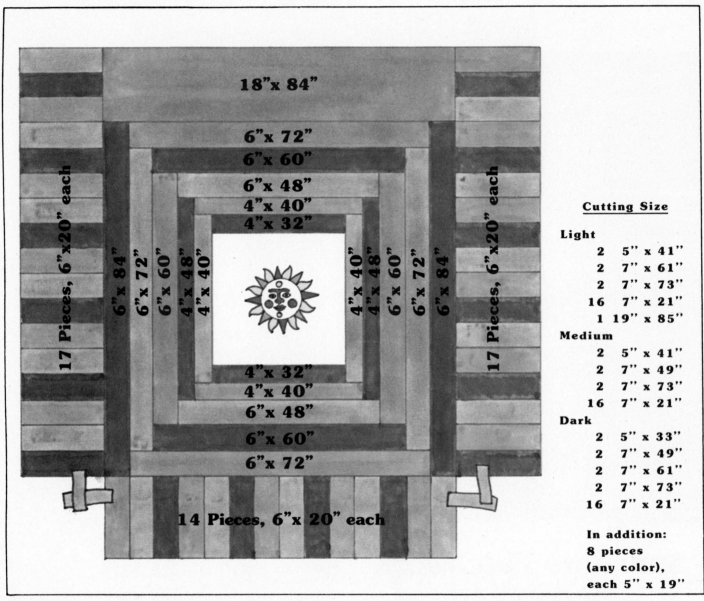

18"x 84"

6"x 72"

6"x 60"

6"x 48"

4"x 40"

4"x 32"

6"x 84"
6"x 72"
6"x 60"
4"x 48"
4"x 40"

4"x 40"
4"x 48"
6"x 60"
6"x 72"
6"x 84"

17 Pieces, 6"x 20" each

17 Pieces, 6"x 20" each

4"x 32"

4"x 40"

6"x 48"

6"x 60"

6"x 72"

14 Pieces, 6"x 20" each

Figure A

<u>Cutting Size</u>

Light

2	5" x 41"
2	7" x 61"
2	7" x 73"
16	7" x 21"
1	19" x 85"

Medium

2	5" x 41"
2	7" x 49"
2	7" x 73"
16	7" x 21"

Dark

2	5" x 33"
2	7" x 49"
2	7" x 61"
2	7" x 73"
16	7" x 21"

**In addition:
8 pieces
(any color),
each 5" x 19"**

4. Cutting sizes for each of the strips are given in **Figure A.** Notice that these sizes are 1 inch longer and 1 inch wider than those indicated on the finished bedspread diagram. That is because there is a ½-inch seam on all sides of each strip. So when they are sewn together, they are 1 inch shorter and 1 inch narrower than the original cut size.

5. In addition to the fabric for the bedspread top you will need the following:

A layer of quilt batting to back the entire bedspread. This may be pieced, but the total dimensions are 124 x 122 inches. An additional piece of batting is required for the center panel, 32 inches square.

Backing material the same size as the finished bedspread. Sheets are fine for this. Sew them together to form a backing, 124 x 122 inches.

Artist's acrylic paint to complete the center panel in the following colors: brown, red/orange, orange, and gold.

A small paint brush.

1 skein of rug yarn to coordinate with the fabric (we used bright orange) and a needle with an eye large enough to accommodate 1 strand of yarn.

Masking tape, scissors, straight pins, sewing thread to match the lightest color of fabric, dressmaker's chalk, iron, ironing board, waxed paper, carbon paper, and pencil.

Completing the center panel

1. Cut 2 pieces of fabric, each 33 inches square.

2. Enlarge the sunshine design given in **Figure B** to full size, and use carbon paper and a soft pencil to transfer it to the center of one of the 33-inch squares.

1 square equals 1″

Figure B

Figure C

3. Paint the sunshine design following the colors shown in Figure B with acrylic paint and a small paint brush. Tips on fabric painting are given in the "Techniques" section at the front of this book.

4. Let the completed center panel dry overnight.

Sewing

1. Place the painted center panel and the matching back wrong sides together, sandwiching a layer of quilt batting between them **(Figure C).** Pin the 3 layers together very firmly. Baste the 3 layers together with long running stitches.

2. Machine stitch just barely past the outside design lines **(Figure B),** then stitch about 2 inches out from the first stitching line. You can mark the second stitching line with chalk if you are not confident enough to stitch freehand.

3. Machine stitch all 4 of the center panel sides, ⅜ inch from the edge.

4. Press the completed center panel with a steam iron on the wrong side.

Figure D

Figure E

Sewing the top

1. Place the center panel right side up on a flat work surface. Pin the 2 shortest patchwork strips (33 inches long) on the top and bottom of the center panel with right sides together **(Figure D).**

2. Sew a ½-inch seam down the length of the strip. Carefully press the seam flat.

3. Add the 2 side panels next. Continue alternating the strips at the top and bottom and then the 2 sides **(Figure E)** until you have added all of the strips called for in the center portion of the bedspread (Figure A).

Sewing the back and side panels

1. A total of 48 pieces, each 7 x 21 inches, are required to construct the panels for the 2 sides and the bottom. Cut the individual pieces and stitch them together in the order shown in Figure A (alternating light, medium, and dark).

2. Sew the completed back and side panels to the center section (Figure A).

Tying the bedspread

1. Place the completed bedspread top over the backing fabric, sandwiching a layer of batting between the 2 pieces. Make sure that all layers are completely flat, since any puckers will show in your finished bedspread. You may wish to place it on the floor to work.

2. Pin all 3 layers together. Begin in the center and work out to all 4 edges.

3. Begin tying on the patchwork strip closest to the center panel. Use a double strand of rug yarn. Take a single stitch through all 3 layers, then tie it on top in a double knot **(Figure F).**

4. Trim the ends of the knot to about 1 inch in length. The ties should be placed at even intervals down the center of each strip. Continue tying each strip, working out to all 4 sides 1 strip at a time.

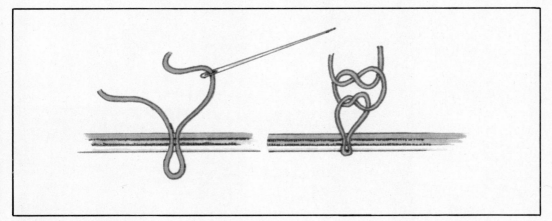

Figure F

Hemming the bedspread

1. Place the bedspread on the bed and smooth it out carefully, making sure that the edges are even all the way around. Mark the bottom and side panels about 1 inch from the floor, using either chalk or straight pins.

2. Cut away all excess fabric, leaving approximately 1½ inches below the mark for a hem allowance.

3. Remove the bedspread from the bed and turn the hem allowance to the wrong side. Press with a steam iron. Machine or hand stitch the hem in place.

4. Repeat the hemming procedure for the backing fabric, hemming it slightly shorter than the front of the bedspread.

Sewing the ties

1. Cut 8 tie pieces, each 5 x 19 inches, from any of the fabric that is left over.

2. Place 2 tie pieces right sides together and sew a ½-inch seam down the long 19-inch side, across the 5-inch end and back up the other 19-inch side **(Figure G)**.

3. Clip the corners and turn the sewn piece right side out. Press with a steam iron.

4. Repeat steps 2 and 3 until you have completed all 4 tie pieces.

5. Fold the raw edges inside on the remaining unstitched end. Press and topstitch the opening closed.

6. Pin 1 tie end on each of the bottom corner sides of the finished bedspread (see Figure A) and topstitch in place.

7. Place the completed bedspread on the bed, and knot the ties loosely.

Figure G

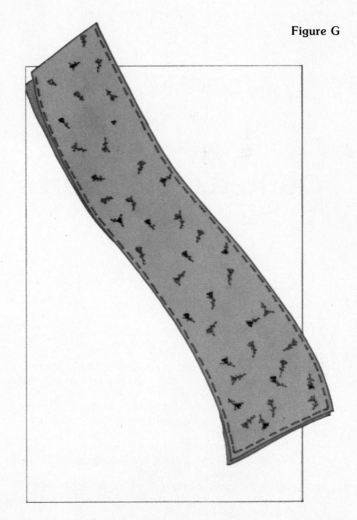

Quilted Owl Pictures

Here's a really different and striking collection to hang on a bare, unnoticed wall. They're traced onto inexpensive bleached muslin with an ordinary laundry marker, machine quilted, and stapled to a plywood square.

Materials

5½ yards of bleached muslin or any similar fabric. If you have smaller pieces of fabric you wish to use, the owls can be made any size you wish.

32 square feet (3½ square yards) of polyester quilt batting.

White sewing thread and straight pins.

Black laundry marker.

Black cotton embroidery thread (optional). Scissors, dressmaker's carbon paper, and a soft pencil.

Iron and ironing board.

Sewing machine (or the project can be done by hand).

Picture frame or a piece of plywood 20 inches square for each of the completed pictures.

Transferring the design

1. Cut the muslin fabric into 8 squares, each 24 inches square. 4 pieces will be the fronts and 4 will be the backs.

2. Enlarge the 4 owl designs given in **Figure A**.

3. Center each of the owl designs on 1 single muslin square. Use a soft pencil and dressmaker's carbon paper to transfer the design to the fabric.

4. After transferring, trace the carbon paper marks with a permanent black laundry marker.

5. An optional step at this point is to add decorative embroidery stitches to the owl designs, such as embroidering the eyes using the satin stitch.

1 square equals 1"

Quilting and framing

1. Pin the design square and backing square wrong sides together, sandwiching a light layer of quilt batting between the 2 layers **(Figure B).**

2. Smooth and pin the 3 layers together, smoothing as you work. Begin pinning in the center of the design and work out to the edges.

3. Machine or hand stitch around the outer edges of each owl, and about ½ inch from all 4 edges of each square.

4. Your finished picture can be framed as any other picture, or (as we did) eliminate the frame and staple the finished picture around a 20-inch square of plywood **(Figure C).** Be sure to miter the corners of the fabric on the back of the plywood to eliminate unwanted bulk.

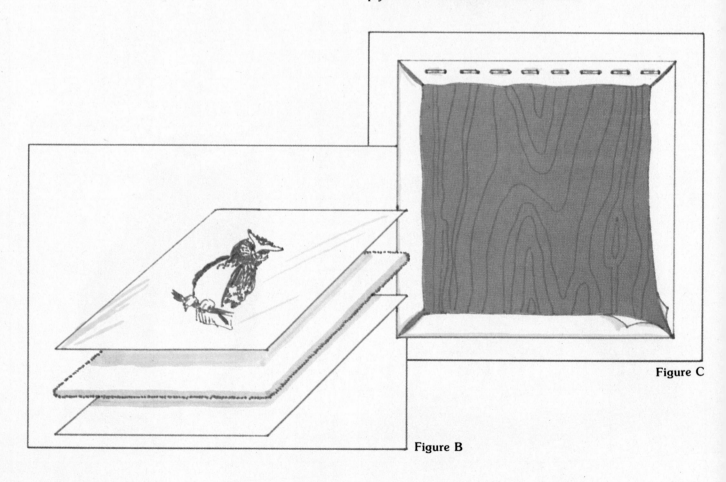

Figure C

Figure B

Forever Calendar

This perpetual calendar can be re-arranged each month and will never be out of date. It's a great way to show off your embroidery skills and use up that leftover embroidery thread. Only four embroidery stitches are required.

Materials

3 yards of off-white linen or other fabric suitable for embroidery.

54 snaps or nylon fastener "spots" for attaching numbers and months to calendar background.

Cotton embroidery thread in the following colors: red, bright green, bright turquoise, bright orange, burnt orange, brown, gold, yellow, tan, black, pink, and light blue. You can, of course, substitute your own choice of colors. It's a great way to use up odds and ends of embroidery thread that you have on hand.

Sewing thread to match the linen fabric.

Embroidery hoop and embroidery needle.

Scissors and straight pins.

Sewing machine (or the project can be finished by hand).

Carpenter's square or T-square.

Dressmaker's carbon paper, tracing paper, and pencil.

 SCORPIO

 APR

NOV

ARIES

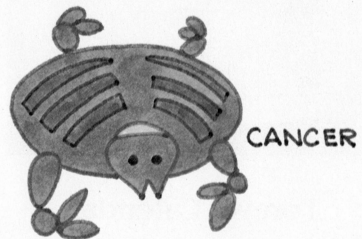 JULY

CAPRICORN

 CANCER

JAN

GEMINI

JUNE

VIRGO

LIBRA

SEPT

OCT

MAY   AUG

TAURUS

LEO

AQUARIUS

FEB

SAGITTARIUS

DEC

MAR

PISCES

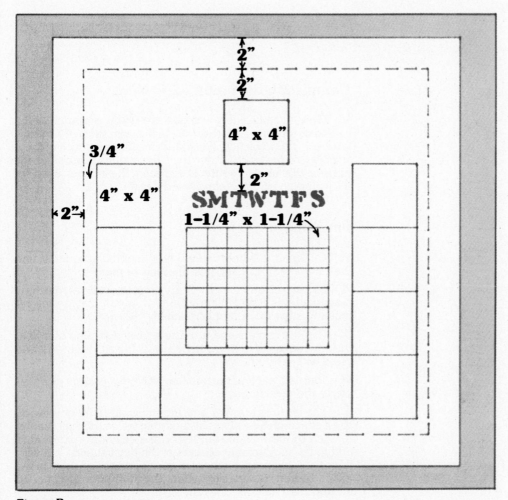

Figure B

Transferring the patterns

1. Trace the patterns given in **Figure A.** Although all of the designs except the numbers are shown in Figure A, the project is worked in 3 separate stages: the background, the calendar month squares, and the numbered day squares. The background consists of the sun and wind designs at the top of the calendar, the outlines for placing the numbered day squares, and the letters on top of the outlines representing the days of the week.

2. The background is completed first. Cut a piece of linen background fabric 27 x 25½ inches. The finished calendar size will be 23 x 21½ inches, so this will allow for a 2-inch border around the entire work.

3. Rule off the outlines for the day squares, referring to **Figure B** when positioning them on the background fabric. Use a carpenter's square or a T-square, as it is most important that they be very square. Your finished project will look lopsided if they are not.

4. Transfer the letters representing the days of the week to the top of the outlines for the day squares.

Transferring the month designs

1. Rule off 24 month squares, each 5 inches square, on the remaining linen fabric (12 fronts and 12 backs). It will make the embroidery work easier if you do not cut apart the squares at this point. The finished months will be 4 inches square, so this will allow a ½-inch seam allowance on all 4 sides.

2. Transfer each of the full-size month designs to the center of a 5-inch square.

Transferring the day squares

1. Rule off 42 squares, each 2 inches square, on the remaining linen fabric. Again, do not cut them apart yet.

2. Full-size patterns for completing the numbers on the day squares are provided in **Figure C.** Transfer 31 numbers to the day squares, combining them for the double-digit days.

3. Transfer the star design in Figure A to the center of the remaining 9 day squares. These will be used to fill in the calendar days not in use that month.

Completing the embroidery work

1. Only 4 embroidery stitches are used to complete the calendar: the long-and-short stitch, the satin stitch, the French knot, and the split stitch. Illustrated directions for each of these stitches are provided under the "Techniques" section at the front of this book. **Figure D** indicates the stitches used for each portion of the embroidered design.

Finishing

1. Cut apart the embroidered month and day squares, and the unworked back squares for each of them.

2. Pin each square right sides together with a matching unworked back, and stitch around 3 edges, leaving the remaining edge open and unstitched.

3. Clip the corners and turn the square right side out. Fold the raw edges of the unstitched opening to the inside and press with an iron.

4. Topstitch each of the squares, stitching as close as possible to the outside edge.

5. The finished number and month squares are now ready to be attached. Sew nylon fastener "spots" to the exact center of each of the outline squares on the calendar background and to the exact center of each of the day squares. It is very important that the placement of each of these "spots" is in the exact center; otherwise, when the numbers are moved around they may be uneven.

6. Repeat the process of sewing nylon fasteners to the back of each of the months, and to the corresponding position on the calendar background.

Framing

1. The completed calendar is now ready for framing. You can use any ordinary picture frame, or stretch the completed work over a 23 x 21½-inch piece of plywood and cover the edges with wood strips, as we did.

2. To use the calendar, place the current month at the top of the calendar and arrange the numbers and star squares to reflect the days for that month.

Figure C

1234567890

Figure D

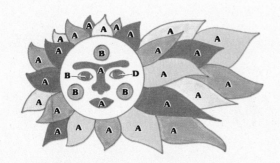

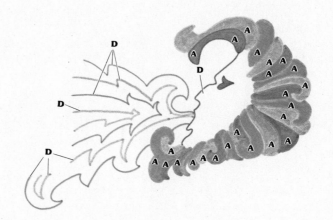

A - Long & Short Stitch
B - Satin Stitch
C - French Knot
D - Split Stitch

SMTWFFS

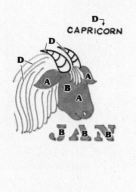
CAPRICORN
JAN

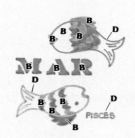
AQUARIUS
FEB

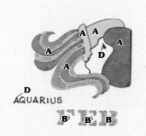
MAR
PISCES

APR
ARIES

MAY
TAURUS

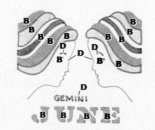
GEMINI
JUNE

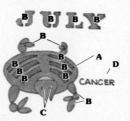
JULY
CANCER

AUG
LEO

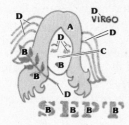
VIRGO
SEPT

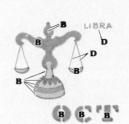
LIBRA
OCT

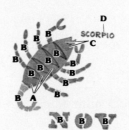
SCORPIO
NOV

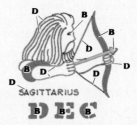
SAGITTARIUS
DEC

107

Latch-Look Flowers

To look at these giant beauties, you'd think they took forever to complete. Not so! The flowers are loops of rug yarn sewn with a sewing machine. The rug-yarn leaves and stems are worked in just one easy embroidery stitch.

Materials

White (or off-white) fabric, 27 x 38 inches, for the background. Choose a fabric with a loose weave so it will be easy to pierce it with a large needle and pull the rug yarn through.
1 skein of rug yarn in each of the following colors: orange, burnt orange, avocado green, chocolate brown, and bright yellow.
Large needle (to accommodate the rug yarn), large embroidery hoop, straight pins, and sewing machine.
Dressmaker's carbon paper, tracing paper, and pencil.

Sewing the "latch-look"

1. Enlarge the flower pattern given in **Figure A,** and transfer it to the center of the background fabric.

2. You may find that placing the fabric in a large embroidery hoop (turned upside down) makes it easier to work on the flowers **(Figure B).**

3. To sew the latch-look flowers, begin by sewing one end of the rug yarn to the fabric **(Figure C).**

4. Loop the yarn so it extends about 1 inch to the left of the presser foot on the sewing machine. Sew straight over the yarn. See **Figure D.**

5. Make another loop to the right of the presser foot, and sew straight over the end of the second loop **(Figure E).**

6. Continue alternating the loops to the left, and then right, until the fabric area is covered. You may work in straight rows back and forth, or in a continuous circle, beginning at the outer design lines and working toward the center of the area. Match the yarn colors to those given in Figure A.

7. When you have finished filling the area, fluff up the loops with your fingers.

8. The leaves, stems, and flower centers are all completed in the satin stitch. Suggested colors are shown in Figure A. Use a large embroidery hoop while working.

Figure A

1 square equals 1″

Figure B

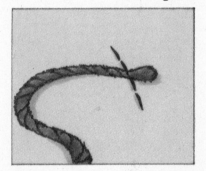

Figure C

Figure D

Figure E

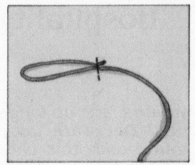

Hospitality Wreath

Wreaths are no longer just for Christmas! Decorate your door all year 'round with this cheerful welcoming message.

Materials

14-inch (inside diameter) styrofoam wreath.
1 yard of yellow calico fabric.
20 x 48-inch piece of quilt batting.
5 yards of 1-inch-wide green satin ribbon.
14-inch-diameter circle of ¾-inch-thick plywood (or substitute 2 layers of heavy cardboard which have been glued together).
Acrylic paint in your choice of colors for the lettering in the center circle. We used bright yellow for the center poem and white for the "Welcome."
If you use plywood for the center circle, you can stain the background with a dark walnut oil stain. If you use cardboard, paint the background with brown acrylic paint.
Very small, good quality artist's paint brush.
Dressmaker's carbon paper and a soft pencil.
Assortment of dried and/or silk flowers. We used 8 silk daisies, 4 dried cornflowers, 2 branches of eucalyptus leaves and a small bunch of baby's breath.
For arranging the flowers you'll also need floral picks, a small styrofoam block (approximately 2 inches square and 1 inch thick).
Floral wire, needle and thread, white glue, 1 foot of picture wire, and straight pins.

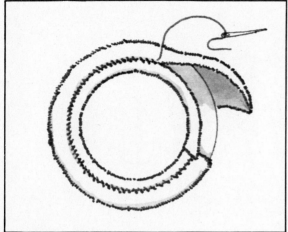

Figure A

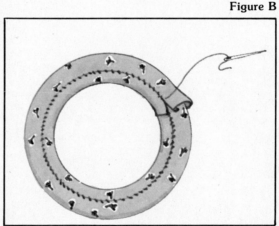

Figure B

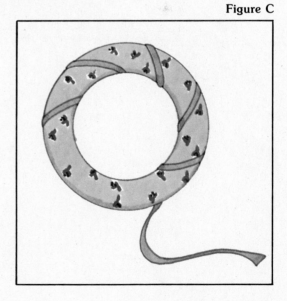

Figure C

Covering the wreath

1. Wrap the styrofoam wreath with a layer of quilt batting to plump it out. Whipstitch the batting together on the back side of the wreath to hold it together **(Figure A).**

2. Cut a piece of calico fabric approximately 10 x 48 inches to cover the wreath. Piece it if necessary.

3. Wrap the fabric over the wreath and batting, overlapping the edges on the back side of the wreath. Use straight pins to hold it in place while you work. Turn the raw edges under and whipstitch them together **(Figure B).**

4. Wrap the green ribbon around the fabric-covered wreath, spacing the wraps about 4 inches apart **(Figure C).** Begin and end at the back of the wreath, whipstitching the ends together.

Completing the center circle

1. If you use a cardboard center, paint the background before beginning work on the lettering. If you are using plywood, stain the background after painting the letters.

2. Full-size letters are provided in **Figure D.** Trace and transfer the letters to the center circle using dressmaker's carbon paper and a soft pencil. Refer to the photo for placement.

3. Paint each of the letters with acrylic paint. Use white paint for the "Welcome" and yellow for the rest of the lettering. Let the finished work dry overnight.

4. If you used plywood, stain the background with a wipe-on oil stain. The oil stain will not adhere to the painted portions of the design. Again, let the work dry overnight.

Welcome

The ornament
of a house
is the friends
who frequent it

~ Emerson

Figure E

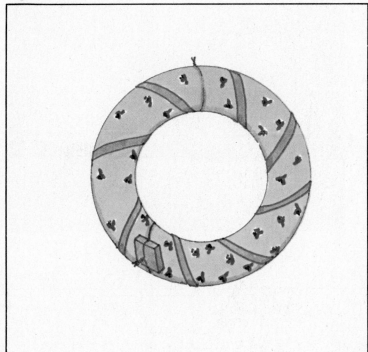

Figure F

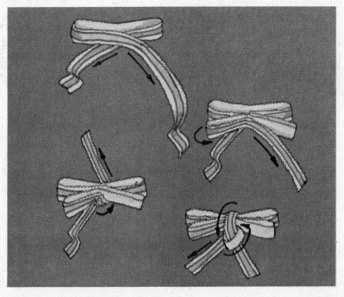

Finishing

1. Wire the styrofoam floral block around the wreath at the lower left. Twist the picture wire around the top of the wreath, pulling it tightly so that it sinks into the wreath and can't be seen **(Figure E).**

2. Wipe glue on the outer edges of the center circle and push it into the center of the fabric-covered wreath. Let the glue dry overnight.

3. Arrange the flowers on the left front of the wreath, pushing the flowers into the styrofoam block. Refer to the photograph for suggested arrangement.

4. To make the ribbon, use pinking shears to cut a 3-inch-wide strip of calico fabric approximately 1½ yards long. Piece the strip if necessary. Sew the green satin ribbon down the center of the calico strip.

5. Tie the ribbon in a bow following the steps given in **Figure F,** and attach it to the front of the floral base to cover any of the styrofoam that is still exposed.

Appliquéd Apple Quilt

This cheerful country quilt is easy to appliqué and stitch up in a minimum of time. The bright red and green colors will work wonders in any room.

Half-apple

Leaf

Apple

Stem

Place on Fold

1 square equals 1"

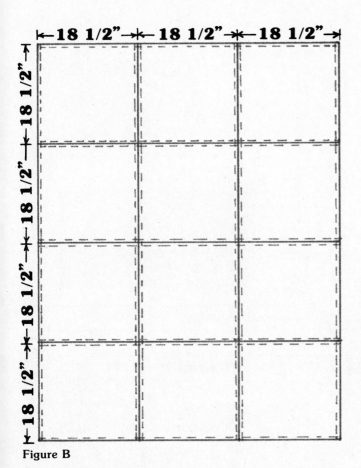

Figure B

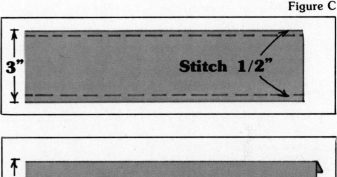

Figure C

Stitch 1/2"

Figure D

Materials

2 white twin sheets for the center section of the quilt (or 2 quilt tops, each 55½ x 74 inches).

6½ yards of pre-quilted green calico fabric.

1½ yards of pre-quilted red calico fabric.

55½ x 74-inch piece of quilt batting.

If you wish to make the matching pillow shams, you'll need extra material. See "Making the Pillow Sham" to figure the amount of fabric necessary for your size pillow.

Sewing needle and thread to match the fabric colors.

Scissors, straight pins, and iron.

Yardstick and tapemeasure.

T-square or carpenter's square.

Dressmaker's chalk in any color except white.

A large flat surface on which to work.

Dressmaker's carbon paper, tracing paper, and pencil.

Cutting the pieces

1. Cut the twin sheets for the center panel to 55½ x 74 inches.

2. Cut the following pieces from pre-quilted green calico: 2 Side Panels, 24 x 81 inches; 1 Bottom Panel, 24 x 55½ inches; 1 Top Panel, 5 x 55½ inches; 3 Horizontal Borders, 3 x 55½ inches; and 2 Vertical Borders, 3 x 74 inches.

3. Patterns for the apples, stems and leaves are given in **Figure A.** Enlarge the patterns to full size and cut 16 stems and 16 leaves from green calico fabric. Cut 8 whole apples and 16 half-apples (8 right and 8 left) from red calico fabric.

Marking the quilt top

1. Iron one center panel piece (twin sheet) and place it right side up on a flat work surface.

2. You will be marking the quilt squares and border areas. It is very important that the lines be marked exactly straight, or the finished quilt will look lopsided.

3. Following **Figure B,** mark the solid lines first, using a carpenter's square or a T-square to make sure your corners are correct.

4. Next mark the dotted lines. The dotted lines that run around the outer edges are 1 inch from the edge and are seam lines that will be used later. All other dotted lines to be marked on the center panel are 1 inch on either side of the solid lines, and will be used to place the horizontal and vertical borders that frame the quilt squares.

Sewing the borders

1. On each of the 3-inch-wide horizontal and vertical border pieces, sew along each long edge, slightly less than ½ inch from the edge (**Figure C**).

2. Fold the stitched edges under on each of the border pieces. They should now be 2 inches wide, with the stitching line no longer visible on the top (**Figure D**). Press with a steam iron.

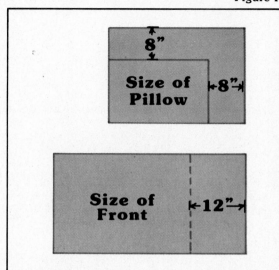

8"

Size of
Pillow
8"

Size of
Front
12"

Figure E

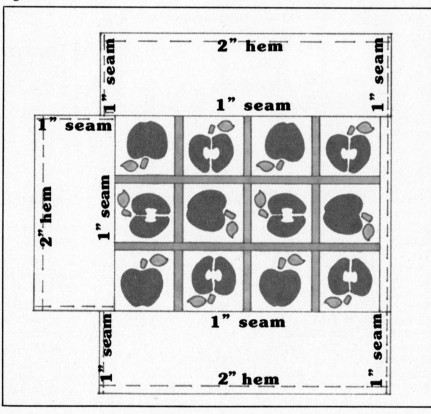

2" hem

1" seam

1" seam

1" seam

1" seam

1" seam

1" seam

2" hem

1" seam

2" hem

1" seam

1" seam

1" seam

1" seam

2" hem

The appliqués

1. Stitch just barely outside the dotted pattern lines on each of the apples, half-apples, stems, and leaves.

2. Turn the outer edges under on each piece so that the stitching is no longer visible. Press with a steam iron.

3. Clip corners and curves so that the appliqué lies flat.

4. Following Figure E, arrange the apples, half-apples, stems, and leaves in the squares. Pin them in place. Baste them to the quilt, ¼ inch from the edges of each piece.

3. Following the layout in **Figure E,** pin the borders to the center panel, following your marked lines. Notice that the vertical borders are attached first, and then covered by the horizontal borders. Baste both sides of each border piece about ¼ inch from the edges.

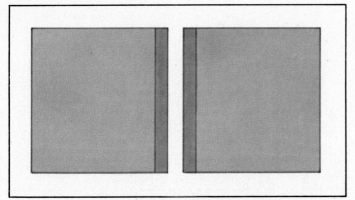

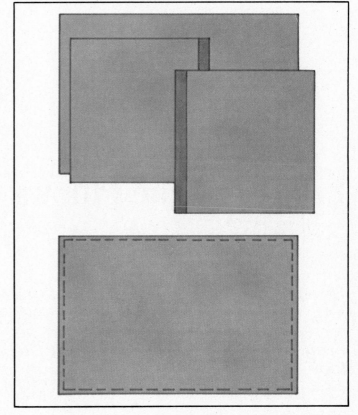

Figure I

Machine stitching

1. Place the remaining plain center panel on your work surface, making sure that it is smooth. Lay the matching quilt batting over it. Then lay the appliquéd center panel on top of the batting, right side up.

2. Pin the 3 layers together securely. Begin pinning in the center, and work out to the 4 sides, smoothing the layers as you work.

3. It will make your sewing and handling of the 3 layers easier if you baste them together at this point. Begin basting in the center and work to the sides.

4. Using matching thread, machine stitch the outside edges of the borders, stems, and leaves. Keep the work flat as you stitch.

5. Change the thread to match, and stitch around the outer edges of each apple and half-apple.

Finishing

1. Pin the top and bottom panels to the center panel, placing right sides together. Stitch a 1-inch seam.

2. Pin the side panels to the center panel, right sides together. Stitch a 1-inch seam.

3. The side panels should be sewn even with the top panel. The excess fabric extends past the bottom of the center panel about 4 inches.

4. Place the quilt on the bed. The pattern hem allowance is 2 inches, but this may be adjusted according to your preference. Pin the hem all the way around, machine stitch, and press.

5. Hand tack the 4-inch excess side panels underneath the bottom panel so that the corners of the bed are covered.

The pillow sham

1. Measure the length and width of your pillow.

2. For each pillow sham, cut 1 front 8 inches longer and 8 inches wider than the pillow measurements **(Figure F)**.

3. Cut the back for the pillow sham 12 inches longer than the front piece.

4. Cut the back piece in half across the width. Sew a 1-inch hem on both sides of the cut **(Figure G)**.

5. Place the front piece right side up. Lay one side of the back piece (wrong side up) on top, matching the raw edges **(Figure H)**. Lay the other side of the back piece (wrong side up) on top of both pieces. The hems will overlap.

6. Machine stitch a 1-inch hem around all 4 outer edges.

7. Clip corners, turn the sham right side out, straighten the corners, and press.

8. Machine stitch around the outside (on the right side) 1 inch from the edges **(Figure I)**.

9. Insert the pillow inside the pillow sham.

Easy Appliqué Pillows

Three bright flower pillows to appliqué and trim with embroidery stitches worked in bold rug yarn. They're as easy to make as they are pretty to look at.

Materials

1 yard each of 36-inch-wide cotton velveteen fabric in the following colors: gold, light brown, green, and red/orange. This will include enough fabric to make the cording around the outer edges of the pillow. Any fabric with a tight weave is suitable; fabric which ravels easily is too difficult to appliqué. If you are using purchased pillows, you probably can use fabric scraps left over from other projects for the flowers themselves.

Small skein of brown rug yarn and a needle large enough to accommodate 1 strand of yarn.

Scissors, brown or black laundry marker, chalk pencil, and thread to match each of the fabric colors.

To make your own pillows requires 2 yards (36 inches wide) of unbleached cotton fabric for pillows back and front. Any similar fabric may be substituted.

5½ yards of ½-inch-diameter cotton cable cord (smaller diameter cord may be substituted.)

3 pillow forms for 14-inch pillows.

Three 12-inch zippers for pillows are optional.

Cutting the pieces

1. Cut 3 squares, each 18 inches square from the cotton fabric. These will be the pillow fronts. Cut 3 squares, each 18 x 20 inches, for the pillow backs. The extra 2 inches allows for the optional zippers to be installed (**Figure A**).

Figure A

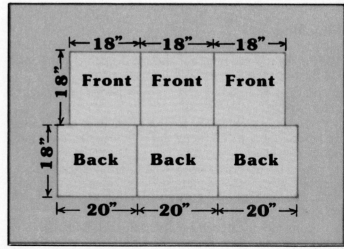

2. Enlarge the patterns in **Figure C** to full size, trace and place them on the velveteen appliqué fabric. Pin patterns in place. If you are planning to use part of the fabric for making cording, keep the appliqué pieces in opposite corners of the fabric. This saves the center of the fabric for cutting the long cording strips, as shown in **Figure B.**

3. Cut each of the appliqué pieces from the fabric, leaving a ⅜-inch seam allowance on the outer edges. Turn the raw edges under, clipping curves and angles as necessary to form a smooth edge. Press with a steam iron. Baste close to edge.

4. The poppy has only 1 appliqué piece. Center the piece on the pillow front and pin in place, as shown in **Figure D.**

5. The tulip stem and leaf should be positioned and pinned on the pillow front first. Then place and pin the tulip flower over the top of the stem.

6. The green sunflower leaf appliqué is centered first on the pillow front and pinned in place. Pin the brown flower appliqué on top of the green leaves. Pin the small gold flower appliqué over the brown flower appliqué. Finish by pinning the red/orange flower center on top.

7. Whipstitch the pinned appliqués to the pillow front, using small hidden stitches.

Figure B

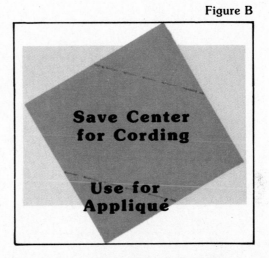

Save Center for Cording

Use for Appliqué

Figure C

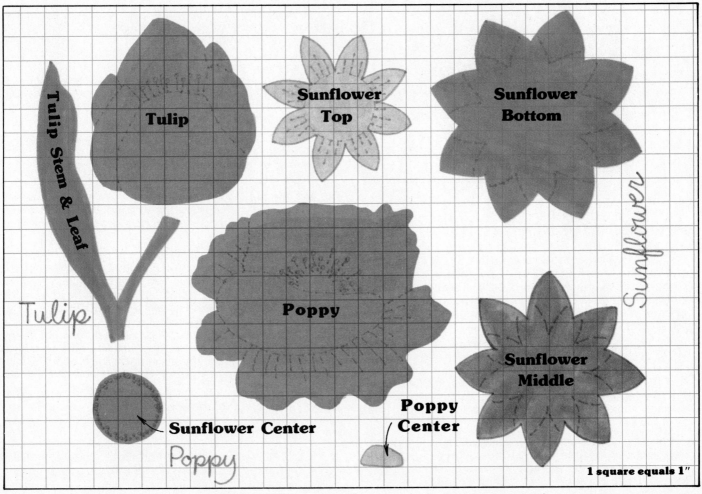

Tulip Stem & Leaf

Tulip

Tulip

Sunflower Top

Sunflower Bottom

Sunflower

Poppy

Sunflower Center

Poppy

Sunflower Middle

Poppy Center

1 square equals 1"

Figure E

Making the pillow

1. Fold the 20-inch side of the pillow backing in half and cut along the fold to form 2 pieces, each 18 inches long and 10 inches wide.

2. Install the 12-inch zipper, as directed on the zipper package, between the two 18-inch edges and press the seams open.

3. To make the cording for the outer border of the pillow, make 6 feet of bias strips. The choice of color is optional. Use a color which coordinates with your pillow appliqué. For small cording, the strips should be a little less than 2 inches wide. For large cording, the strips should be about 2½ inches wide. Fold the unused appliqué fabric so a crosswise edge is parallel to a long edge. The fold line will be the true bias. Cut along that line; then cut bias strips parallel to it until you have a total length of about 6 feet.

4. Stitch the strips together to make a single continuous length. Always seam along the straight grain of the fabric when you join the bias strips. The seam may look strange, but pressing straightens it, as shown in **Figure E.**

5. Lay the cording in the center of the wrong side of the bias strip. Then fold the edges of the strip together. Use a zipper foot on your sewing machine to enclose the cord in the strip as snugly as possible.

6. Place the finished pillow front right side up on a flat surface. Pin the finished cording around the outside of the worked pillow front, with the cord edge facing in toward the center and the raw edge facing out. Overlap the ends of the cording where they meet and stitch along their outer edge through all the layers, including the pillow front. The outer edges should each measure 14 inches. To eliminate floppy corners on the finished pillow, gradually taper the cording in toward the center so the middle of each side is about ½ inch fuller than the corners, making all 4 sides bow out slightly.

7. Place the pillow back with the right side down and the zipper open on top of the pillow front and cording. Pin it in place. Stitch around the outside edge, through the pillow backing, cording and front.

8. Trim all the edges to ½ inch and clip the corners. Turn the pillow right side out and press it with a steam iron. Insert the pillow form and zip it up.

Figure D

Embroidery and padding

1. Only 2 embroidery stitches are used. These are the split stitch and the French knot. Embroider broken lines on the pattern pieces with the split stitch. All circles should be covered with a French knot. The embroidery is done with brown rug yarn. When embroidering, sew entirely through the appliqué and the backing fabric.

2. To create a padded look for each flower, slit the wrong side of the completed pillow front underneath each separate flower section. (A flower section would be 1 petal or portion of a leaf which has been embroidered or whipstitched on all sides.) Just a short slit will do it. Gently push polyester fiberfill into each section until it fills out on the front side. Then whipstitch the opening closed.

3. Write the flower name on the pillow front using a chalk pencil, as shown in Figure D. When the chalk writing looks the way you want it, either embroider it with the split stitch, or retrace it with a black or brown laundry marker.

THE CLOTHES  HANGER
unique projects to wear or carry

Patchwork Party Skirt

Very little sewing is required to complete this versatile skirt. Use up all those gorgeous pieces of fabric that you have been saving. The skirt can be worn with a casual blouse for an evening at home, or topped with a dressy blouse for a night on the town.

Materials

1 pair of worn-out pants with a good waistband and zipper.
Scraps of fabric in bright colors. Choose fabrics of similar weight; combining light and heavy fabrics may cause the finished skirt to hang unevenly.
2½ yards of 45-inch-wide plain white cotton lining fabric.
2½ yards of 45-inch-wide iron-on fusible material.
One package of extra-wide hem (or seam) tape.
Embroidery thread and needle to accommodate the thread. If you use heavy wool fabrics for your patchwork, the embroidery work should be done with a lightweight yarn. If you use lightweight cottons, use cotton embroidery thread.
An embroidery hoop.
Yardstick, sewing thread, sewing machine, tailor's chalk, and scissors.

Figure A

Figure B

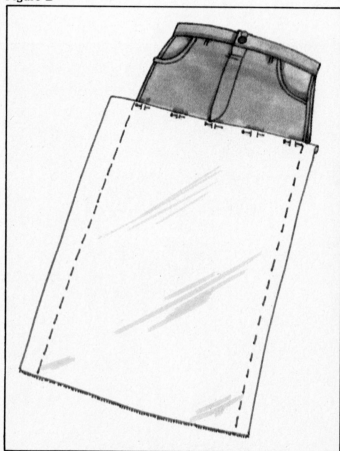

Laying out the pattern

1. Cut off the top of the pants, just below the zipper fly (**Figure A**).

2. Cut two 36 x 45-inch pieces of lining fabric. Turn under a 1-inch-wide seam allowance across one 36-inch edge, and press.

3. Pin the hemmed edge to the pants just below the fly, straight across the pants.

4. With pencil or chalk and yardstick, draw a line from the side seam of the pants to ½ inch from the selvage edge at the bottom of the fabric (**Figure B**).

5. Cut out the resulting front lining, adding a ½-inch seam to the sides of the marked lines.

6. Remove the front lining from the pants, and use it as a pattern to cut a matching back lining.

7. Cut 2 matching pieces of iron-on fusing material the same size as the front and back lining pieces. Pin the fusing material on top of 1 lining piece.

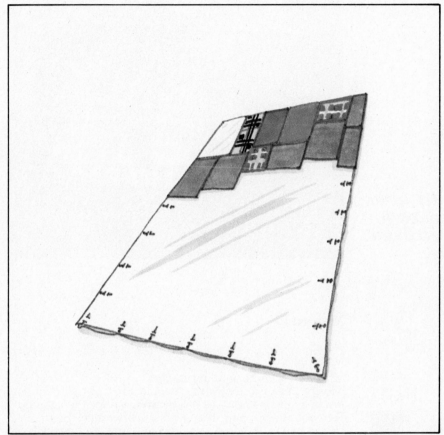

Figure C

Adding the pieces

1. Place the lining (with the fusible material on top) on a flat work surface. Begin cutting and placing fabric scraps on top of the fusible material in a crazy-quilt pattern **(Figure C)**. There is no specific pattern; simply fit the cut pieces together as you wish, working from the top of the lining down to the bottom. Use an iron to fuse each of the pieces to the lining as you work. Overlap some pieces on the top and sides of the fusible material. Be sure that the pieces are fused together carefully at the points where they meet, and that no lining or fusible material shows through between the patches. Repeat the process on the back lining.

2. When both the front and back lining pieces are completely covered with fused patches, place them right sides together and sew down the side seams with a large basting stitch.

3. Baste the completed lining pieces to the pants top just below the fly and try the skirt on. Correct the fit if necessary,

and mark the hemline. Because of the bulkiness of the finished skirt, we suggest that the hem not be turned under, but rather the bottom hem be faced with either extra-wide hem tape or a fabric facing that you cut from the lining material.

4. After you have determined that the skirt fits well, permanently stitch the side seams and stitch the skirt to the pants top.

5. To tie the pants top and the patchwork skirt together visually, cut additional patches and matching pieces of fusible material. Place these additional patches over the pockets, flush with the patches at the top of the skirt. Fuse them in place with an iron.

6. To complete your skirt, embroider over each of the lines between patches using the feather stitch. Illustrated instructions for this stitch are given in the "Tips and Techniques" section at the beginning of this book.

7. Trim the bottom of the skirt, attach the fabric facing or seam tape, and hem by hand.

Jiffy Backpack

A child will be delighted with your present of a brand new backpack for school or biking. There's no need to tell anyone how easy it is to make.

Figure A

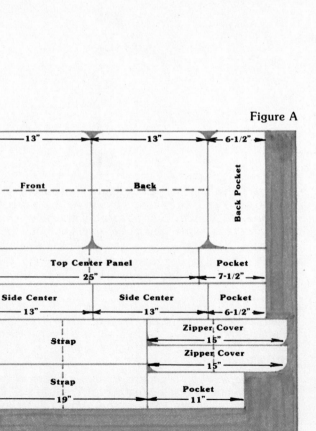

Materials

1 yard of 36-inch-wide canvas (or substitute any sturdy fabric).
12- or 14-inch heavy-duty zipper.
Sewing thread to match the fabric color.
White acrylic paint and small paint brush for the lettering.
Scissors, straight pins, iron, and a sewing machine.
Dressmaker's carbon paper, tracing paper, and pencil.

Sewing the center panel

1. Enlarge, transfer, and cut the pattern pieces given in **Figure A.**

2. Following the manufacturer's instructions printed on the package, install the zipper in the middle of the Top Center Panel (**Figure B**).

3. Place 2 Zipper Covers right sides together, and stitch around the outer edges, leaving seam unstitched between small circles (**Figure C**).

4. Clip corners and curves, and turn the zipper cover right side out. Press, turning the edges on the seam opening to the inside.

5. Center the zipper cover over the zipper and pin it in place (**Figure D**). Topstitch along the straight edge of the cover.

6. With right sides together, match notches and sew Side Center Panels to each end of the Top Center Panel (**Figure E**).

Figure B

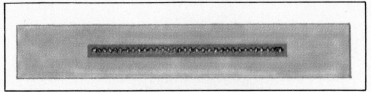

Figure C

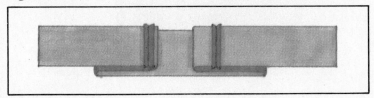

Figure D

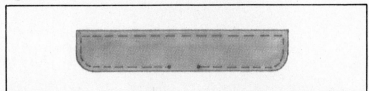

Figure E

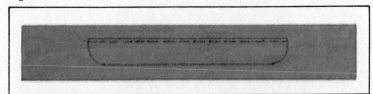

Figure F

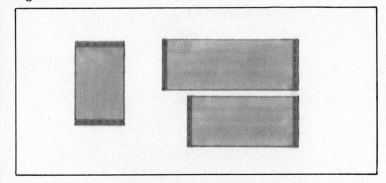

Figure G

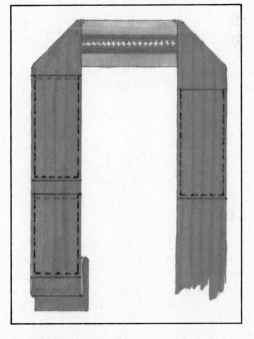

Figure H

7. Hem the top and bottom edges of all 3 pockets **(Figure F)**.

8. Sew pockets to right side of center panel **(Figure G)**. Exact placement is optional on all pockets, but bear in mind that the center 12 inches of the panel will be at the top of the finished backpack.

Painting and sewing the back

1. Hem the top edge of the Back Pocket, and place it on top of the Back. Stitch around 2 sides and across the bottom, ¼ inch from the outer edges **(Figure H)**.

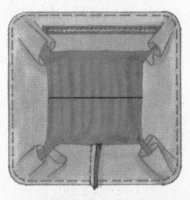

Figure J

Figure K

Figure L

Figure I

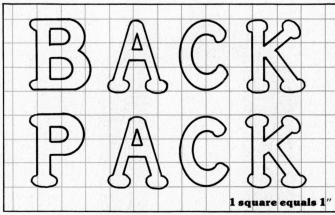

1 square equals 1"

2. Enlarge the "back pack" letters given in **Figure I** to full size and transfer them to the backpack, centering them as shown in the photo.

3. Paint the letters with white acrylic paint. Tips on fabric painting are given in the front of this book under the "Techniques" section.

4. After you have finished, let the paint dry overnight before completing the sewing.

Finishing

1. With right sides together, pin and then sew the Center Panel to the Back piece **(Figure J)**.

2. Sew the 2 free ends of the Center Panel together at the bottom of the backpack. Clip seams on the corner curves.

3. Pin remaining back piece to the unstitched edges of the center panel, with right sides together. Stitch **(Figure K)**.

4. Turn the backpack right side out through the zipper opening.

5. Fold the strap piece in half lengthwise. Fold the raw edges on the sides and the ends to the inside and press with an iron **(Figure L)**. Topstitch around all edges.

Figure M

6. Fit the straps to your child at this point. Pin the straps in place. Twist the straps as shown to fit the child's shoulders **(Figure M)**. It looks strange, but it works! Adjust the strap length as necessary and triple-stitch in place for strength.

128

Folk Art Blouse

Combine bits and pieces of fabric to create this charming blouse. Reminiscent of Early American folk art, it's a beautiful way to show off your creative skills.

Materials

1 yard of iron-on fusing material 36 inches wide.

Scraps of calico, small prints, or light weight solid color fabric.

Pullover blouse in any solid color.

Plain paper, dressmaker's carbon paper, and a pencil.

Scissors, straight pins, and sewing machine (or complete the edging on the appliqués by hand).

Iron and ironing board.

Yellow cotton embroidery thread to embroider the sun's rays and other brightly colored threads if you plan to edge the appliqués by hand. If you machine stitch the appliqués, use regular sewing thread in bright colors.

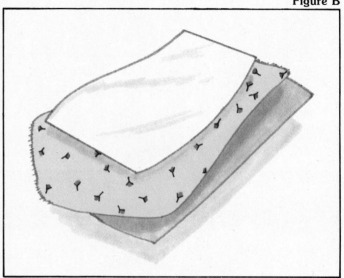

Cutting the pieces

1. Enlarge the background design in **Figure A** to full size on a piece of plain paper.

2. Cut apart the paper pattern to separate the individual background pieces.

3. Place each individual paper pattern right side up on a scrap of fabric (follow the colors given in Figure A). Slip a layer of iron-on fusing material underneath the fabric, and securely pin all 3 layers together **(Figure B).** Cut out, carefully following the pattern lines.

4. Enlarge the foreground designs in **Figure C** to full size. Transfer these designs to fabric scraps. Place a matching piece of iron-on fusing material underneath designs and cut out.

Figure A

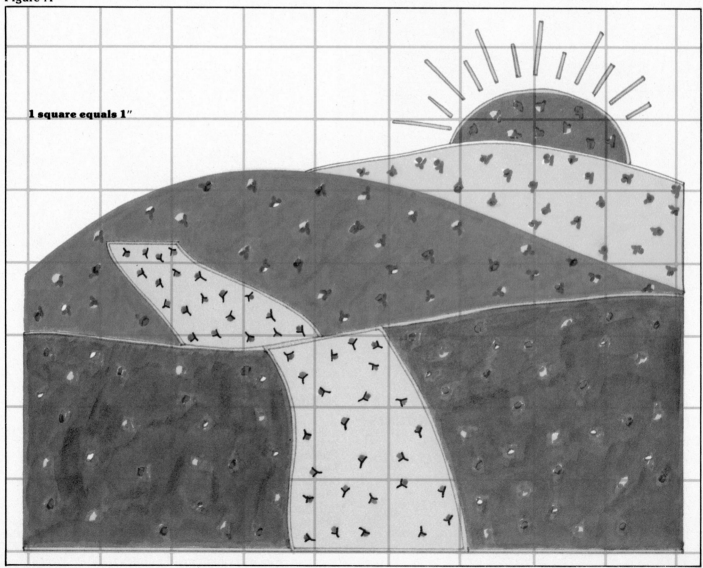

1 square equals 1″

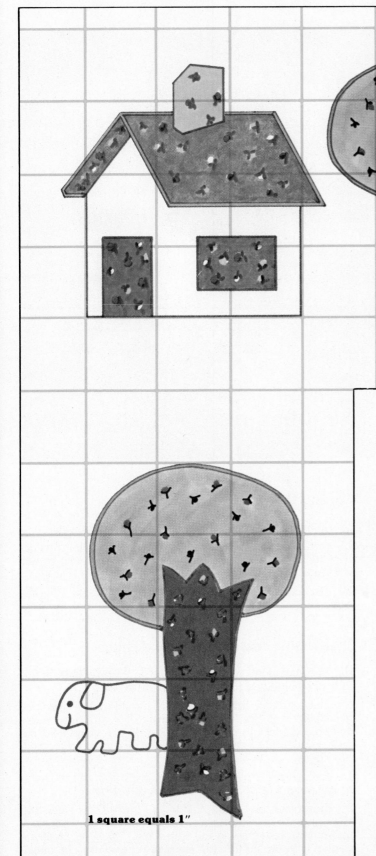

Figure C

1 square equals 1″

Fusing the appliqués

1. Place the blouse on the ironing board and smooth and straighten the blouse front.

2. Carefully remove the paper pattern from each of the background fabric pieces, leaving the fusing material still pinned to the back.

3. Reassemble the complete background design on the blouse front. If the design extends past the side seams on the blouse, you can trim the sides of the appliqué pieces where they meet the seam. Pin the reassembled pieces to the blouse front. Be sure that the raw edges of the separate pattern pieces fit together closely.

4. Beginning at the top of the design, gently iron the assembled background, following the manufacturer's instructions for using the fusing material. Work carefully, making sure that all raw edges are securely fused together.

5. Repeat the procedure (steps 3 and 4) for the foreground pieces (Figure C), fusing them in their proper positions on top of the assembled background.

6. Machine or hand stitch around all edges on each of the pattern pieces in the design. Use a zig-zag stitch (fairly wide and close together) if you are using a machine; a satin stitch if you are hand embroidering. Illustrated embroidery stitch instructions are provided in the "Tips and Techniques" section at the beginning of this book. Change thread colors throughout the work to add interest to the picture.

7. The last step is to embroider the rays of the sun with yellow embroidery thread and a simple chain stitch.

8. Press the completed needlework on the wrong side.

131

Initialed Canvas Purse

Accent any outfit from jeans to dresses with this stylish tote. The black-and-brown flowered initial will complement any outfit.

Materials

⅝ yard of 30-inch-wide heavy muslin, light canvas fabric, or similar fabric.

½ yard of small cotton print fabric for the lining.

2 wooden purse handles, each 12 inches long, with slots in each end to accommodate the fabric straps. These can be purchased in most hobby or craft stores.

Sewing thread to match the purse fabrics.

One skein each of brown and black cotton embroidery thread. Sewing machine, iron, embroidery needle, embroidery hoop, and straight pins.

Dressmaker's carbon paper, tracing paper, and pencil.

Cutting the pieces

1. Enlarge the pattern shown in **Figure A** to full size.

2. Cut 2 each of the Purse Body and Strap pattern pieces from the muslin or canvas fabric. The pattern layout is shown in **Figure B.**

3. Cut 2 lining pieces from the cotton print fabric, using the Purse Body pattern.

Completing the embroidery designs

1. Alphabet patterns are provided in **Figure C.** Choose your 2 initial letters and enlarge them to full size.

2. The leaf and flower design is provided full size. Use dressmaker's carbon paper to transfer it to the front Purse Body piece. Place the bottom of the design 3 inches from the lower edge of the fabric, centering the design between the 2 side edges.

3. Transfer the 2 initials to the center portion of the flower design (refer to photograph of the finished purse).

4. Embroider the design, following **Figure D** for stitch and color placement. The entire design is outlined with black embroidery thread using the split stitch. The solid areas are worked with brown thread using the satin stitch. The initials are worked with the black thread in the satin stitch.

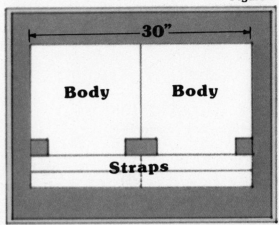

Figure B

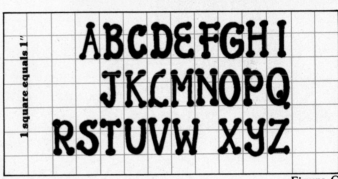

Figure C

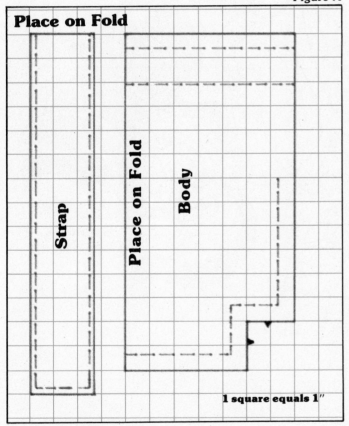

Figure A

Place on Fold

Strap

Place on Fold

Body

1 square equals 1"

1 square equals 1"

Sewing the purse

1.   Press the finished embroidery gently on the wrong side using a steam iron.

2.   Sew darts at the bottom of the purse body by bringing right sides of the 2-inch cutouts together (matching notches), and sewing a ⅝-inch seam.

3.   Sew the 2 purse body pieces right sides together across the bottom and up the side seams. Leave a 6-inch opening at the top of each side seam.

4.   Sew the lining pieces together following steps 2 and 3.

5.   Turn the purse body right side out and insert the lining inside the body, with wrong sides together, as shown in **Figure E**.

6.   Turn the top seam allowances on both the purse and lining to the inside and stitch across the top, stitching through both the purse and lining.

7.   Turn the top edges of the purse to the inside along the casing allowance line and press. Stitch across the casing allowance line to form a casing for the purse handles, as shown in **Figure F**.

8.   Stitch the ends of the strap pieces together, forming 1 continuous 60-inch strap, as shown in **Figure G**.

9.   Fold the raw edges of the strap to the inside along the seam allowance and press. Topstitch both edges of the strap. Fold the raw ends to the inside and topstitch, as shown in **Figure H** and **Figure I**.

10.   Insert the wooden purse handles through the casing. Thread the strap through the slots in the handles. Tie the ends. Shorten the straps if desired.

133

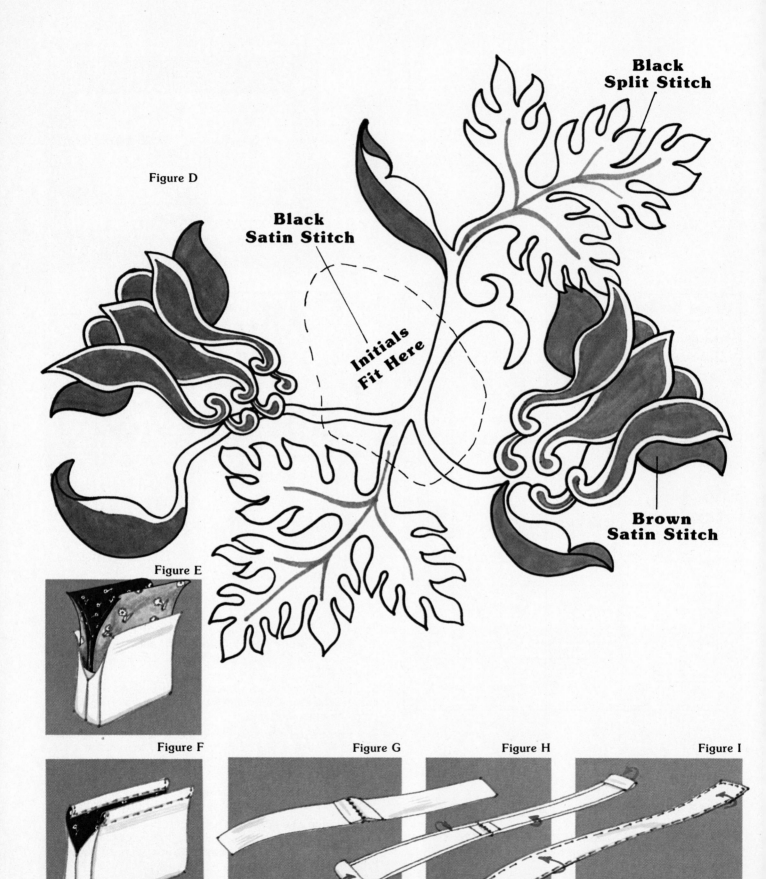

Figure D

Black
Satin Stitch

Black
Split Stitch

Initials
Fit Here

Brown
Satin Stitch

Figure E

Figure F

Figure G

Figure H

Figure I

Save and Sew Wraparound Skirt

This is a marvelous way to use up all those remnants and pieces of expensive trim that were too large to throw away, but not big enough to make anything. Choose colors to mix and match with existing tops and create a whole new wardrobe.

Materials

Both of these skirts are made from the same pattern; each contains 12 different panels (or gores) which are narrow at the top and wider at the bottom.

View A (left model in photo) is assembled from old jean pant legs. You should be able to cut 2 skirt gores from each pant leg, so you will need 6 pant legs to make the skirt. View B (right model in photo) is assembled from fabric remnants. As many as 12 different fabrics may be used. When choosing fabrics, select all 12 in coordinating colors (any combination of solids, prints, and stripes which contain the same basic colors — such as yellows, pinks and greens). Choose the same or similar weights of fabric (all cotton, for example). Mixing very heavy and very light fabrics in a skirt will cause the gores to hang unevenly.

Whatever your choice of fabric, make sure that it is preshrunk, as different fabrics may shrink at different rates and cause puckers in the finished skirt.

Scissors, straight pins, thread to match fabric, sewing needle, and (for View B only) short lengths of trim, ribbon, rick-rack, and lace in coordinated colors.

Iron and ironing board.

Dressmaker's carbon paper, tracing paper, and pencil.

Cutting the patterns

1. Enlarge the skirt Gore and Waistband patterns in **Figure A** to full size. The top of the skirt gore pattern has 3 lines: small (sizes 8-10), medium (sizes 12-14) and large (sizes 16-18). Cut the top of the pattern on the line indicated for your size.

2. Check the hem length before cutting and shorten or lengthen the pattern to fit. To lengthen, extend the side cutting lines in a continuous straight line.

3. Place the enlarged patterns on the fabric following the straight grain marking (←→), and cut out. Cut 12 Gore pieces and 4 Waistband pieces. If you wish, you can use several different fabrics for the waistband. In the case of View B, we substituted grosgrain ribbon for the tie ends of the waistband.

Figure B

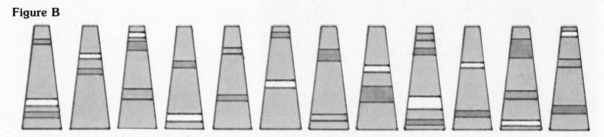

Figure A

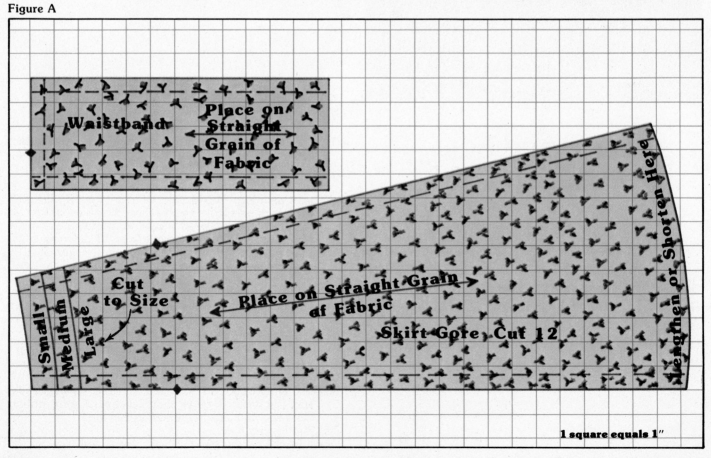

Waistband

Place on Straight Grain of Fabric

Small
Medium
Large

Cut to Size

Place on Straight Grain of Fabric

Skirt Gore Cut 12

Lengthen or Shorten Here

1 square equals 1"

136

Sewing the skirt

1. Any short length of ribbon, lace, rick-rack, seam binding, or bias tape may be used to trim the individual gores (View B). Pin the trim in place across the individual gores in an irregular pattern. **Figure B** is a suggested layout pattern for trim, but feel free to place your trim wherever you wish. Use the short pieces of trim at the top of the gore, and the longer pieces across the bottom. You can also leave some gores untrimmed. Sew each trim piece to the gore before sewing the gores together.

2. Stitch the 12 skirt gores together at the side seams allowing a ⅝-inch seam, as shown in **Figure C.** You may wish to lay out the sequence of gores before stitching them together. Press all seams open. Staystitch around the waist edge.

3. Wrap the sewn gores around your waist, and check the skirt length before hemming. Remember that a ⅝-inch seam allowance should be above your waistline to allow for attaching the waistband. Hem side edges, first pressing under ¼ inch on edges, then pressing the turned edges to inside along seam line. Machine or hand stitch the side edges.

4. With right sides together, pin and stitch the waistband pieces together, as shown in **Figure D.** Press seams open.

Figure C

Figure D

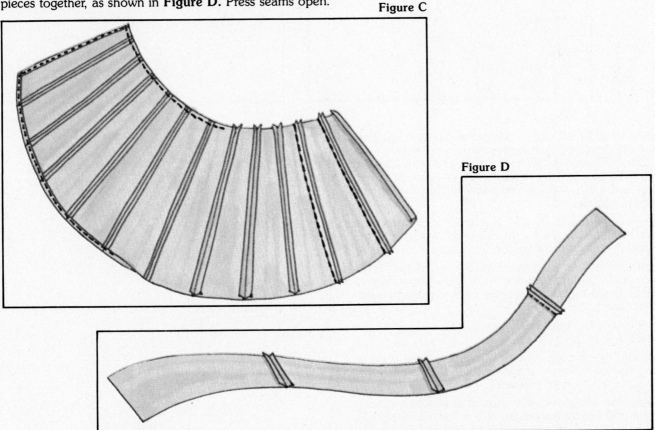

137

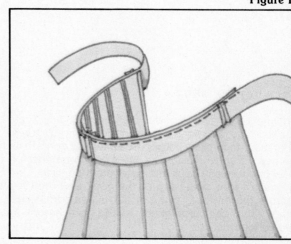

Figure E

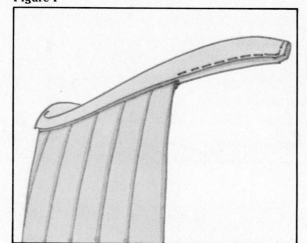

Figure F

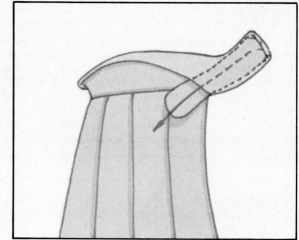

Figure G

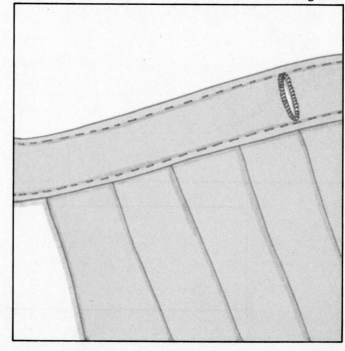

Figure H

5. Pin seamed waistband to skirt waist placing right sides together and matching center seam of skirt and center seam of waistband **(Figure E)**. Stitch seam, trim and press it toward waistband. At this point, if you wish to use ribbon you can cut the waistband even with the side edges of the skirt top and sew ribbon to replace it.

6. Fold the waistband in half lengthwise with right sides together. Machine stitch to the point where the skirt attaches to waistband, as shown in **Figure F.** Trim seams and corners.

7. Turn ends of waistband right side out and press **(Figure G)**. Press under seam allowance on remaining raw edge of waistband. On the inside, whipstitch pressed edge of waistband over seam.

8. On right side, topstitch ¼ inch from edges of the waistband.

9. By hand or machine, work a buttonhole large enough to accommodate the ends of the waistband (above the 4th seam in skirt), as shown in **Figure H.**

10. Wrap the completed skirt around your waist, passing the left tie end through the buttonhole in the waistband. Tie in front.

11. Mark the hemline, trim to 1½ inches in width, and press the hem to the wrong side. Hand stitch the hem.

138

Lady Bug Appliqué

We attached this bright and cheerful appliqué design to a white caftan, but it can be stitched up in any size, and attached to a child's dress, a pillow, or an apron front.

Materials

Fabric scraps in bright colors for the appliqués.
Clothing item in a coordinating solid color.
Embroidery thread in colors to complement the fabric colors.
Embroidery needle and embroidery hoop (or you can use a
    zig-zag stitch on a sewing machine).
1 yard of iron-on fusing material.
Scissors, straight pins, iron, and ironing board.
Dressmaker's carbon paper, tracing paper, and pencil.

Cutting the pieces

1. Enlarge the pattern pieces for the tulip, leaf, and lady bug **(Figure A)** to full size.

2. Transfer each of the enlarged pattern pieces to fabric, and cut out carefully. Cut 2 complete lady bugs. The spots on the lady bug are appliquéd on top of the body.

3. Cut a piece of iron-on fusing material the exact size of each of the pattern pieces.

4. Place the appliqué pieces on the clothing, referring to the photograph for suggested placement. When you have an arrangement you like, pin the pieces in place, placing a matching piece of fusing material underneath the appliqué **(Figure B)**.

139

Figure A

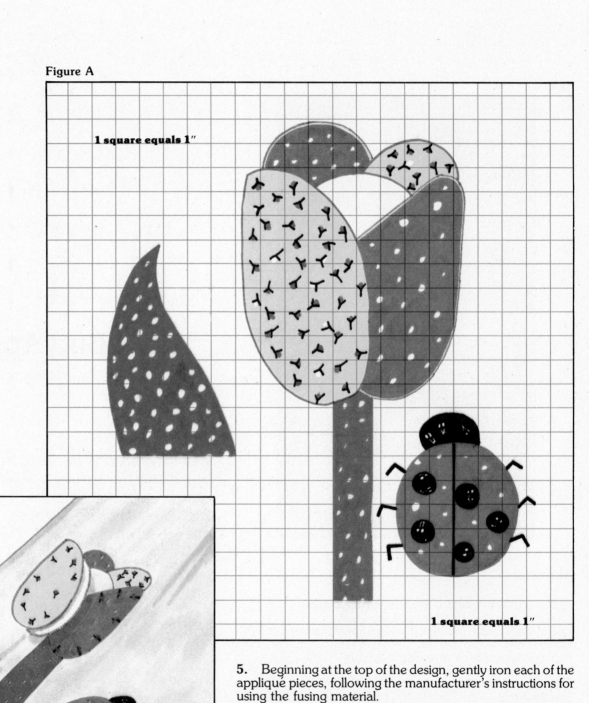

1 square equals 1"

1 square equals 1"

Figure B

5. Beginning at the top of the design, gently iron each of the appliqué pieces, following the manufacturer's instructions for using the fusing material.

6. Machine or hand stitch around each of the appliqué pieces. Use a zig-zag stitch (fairly wide and close together) if you are using a machine; a satin stitch if you are hand embroidering. Illustrated embroidery stitches are provided in the "Tips and Techniques" section at the beginning of this book. Change thread colors throughout the work to add interest to the design.

7. Gently press the completed needlework on the wrong side.

THE GIFT BOX
great gifts and bazaar items

Calico Baskets

You can stitch up these baskets in double-quick time with a minimum of materials. Use them to hold small green plants, artificial flowers, biscuits, and bread. Or, line them with a plastic refrigerator storage container and fill them with munchies for a party.

Materials

For each basket you will need two 15-inch squares of fabric, one for the outside of the basket and one for the inside. These pieces do not have to be of the same fabric; two coordinated materials would look great. We do suggest that you use calico or other small prints, as large prints will overwhelm the basket design.

One 15-inch-square piece of lightweight inner lining fabric. The color is not important as long as it will not show through the printed fabric used for the basket. We suggest that you use white or some other light color.

One 15-inch-square piece of 6-ply quilt batting.

If you plan to make a handle on the basket, you need 2 additional pieces of print fabric, 1 piece each of underlining and 1 piece of quilt batting, each 3 x 14 inches; and an ordinary coat hanger to stiffen the handle.

28-inch length of lace trim (optional) and ribbon for a tying bow on the completed basket.

Sewing thread to match or coordinate with the print fabric.

Tracing paper and a soft pencil.

Wire cutters (to cut the coat hanger).

Scissors, sewing needle, sewing machine (or the basket can be completed by hand), and straight pins.

Cutting the pieces

1. A full-size pattern for the basket is given in **Figure A**. Transfer it to tracing paper, marking the "place on fold" notations on the 2 straight sides. To cut the outside basket piece, fold the 15-inch square of print fabric in quarters and pin together so that it will not slip **(Figure B)**. Place the full-size basket pattern on top of the folded print square, making sure that the "place on fold" notations are indeed on both folded edges of the fabric square. Pin the pattern to the fabric and cut out.

2. Cut the inside basket from the print fabric, the basket underlining, and a layer of batting in the same manner as you did for the outside basket piece.

3. If you wish to add a handle to the basket, cut 2 fabric handle pieces, 1 inner lining piece and 1 quilt batting piece from the full-size pattern shown in Figure A. Again, pay particular attention to the "place on fold" notations given on the pattern.

Place on Fold

Strap

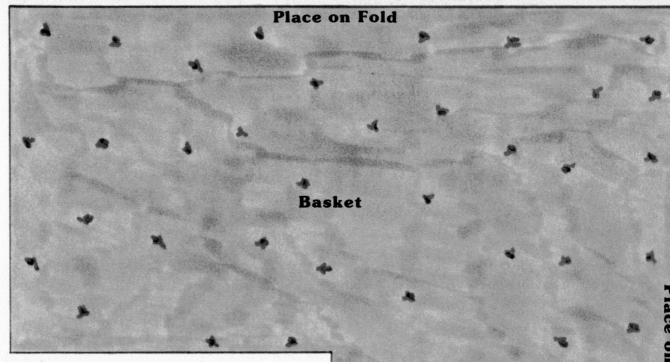

Place on Fold

Basket

Place on Fold

Figure A

Sewing the basket

1. Place the basket underlining right side up on your work surface. Place the batting on top. Over that, place the inner and outer basket pieces, with right sides facing each other. Carefully pin the pieces together **(Figure C).**

2. Sew a ½-inch seam around the edges, sewing through all 4 layers. Leave one of the edges open and unstitched between the dots as shown in Figure C.

3. Turn the stitched basket right side out, and press with a steam iron.

4. Topstitch a square in the center of the basket, as shown in **Figure D,** double stitching for strength.

5. An optional step at this point is to sew across each of the basket sides. The beige calico basket sides were stitched; the sides of the yellow basket were not.

6. Turn the remaining raw edges to the inside and whipstitch them together. If you plan to add a handle to your basket, leave a 3-inch-wide center opening **(Figure E).**

7. Fold up each of the 4 basket sides and whipstitch each corner together, working from the top of the basket down **(Figure F).**

144

Figure B

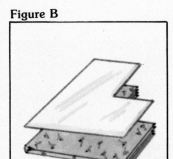

Figure C

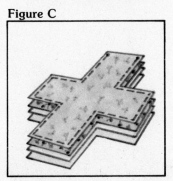

Figure D

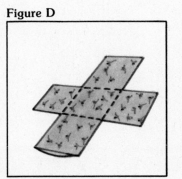

Figure E

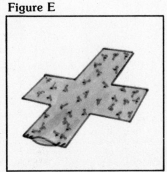

Figure F

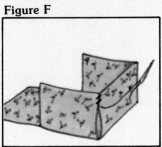

Figure G

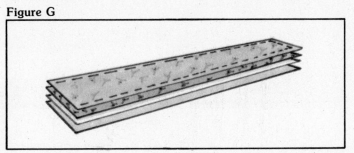

Figure H

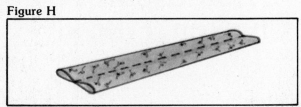

Figure I

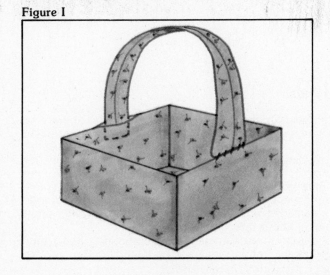

Adding the lace and handles

If you do not plan to add a handle to your basket, skip down to step 6.

1. The handle is sewn in the same layers as was the basket; first the inner lining, then the quilt batting, and lastly the 2 fabric pieces (placed right sides together). Carefully pin the 4 layers together, and begin stitching at one narrow end of the handle. Sew a ½-inch seam down the side, across the end, and back up the other side of the handle **(Figure G).**

2. Turn the handle right side out and press with a steam iron.

3. Topstitch down the center of the handle, sewing through all layers **(Figure H).**

4. Cut a piece of coat hanger the same length as the completed handle. Insert the coat hanger inside the handle.

5. Whipstitch the raw edges of the fabric handle inside the 3-inch opening which you left in the side of the basket **(Figure I).** Whipstitch the sewn end of the handle to the top of the opposite basket side.

6. Whipstitch the lace or other trim around the top edges of the basket, allowing a generous amount of lace at each corner.

7. Tie a coordinating bow on the handle side, if desired.

Homespun Chicken Pillow

Although we made this pillow to use in a kitchen sitting area, it would roost most comfortably in any room in your home. Recycle an old tired cushion by attaching this bright new appliquéd front – or sew the entire pillow.

Materials

You can stitch up the pillow front and attach it to an existing 13-inch square, or combine it with a pillow you make yourself. If you plan to make the pillow, you will need the following materials: a 15-inch-square piece of fabric for the pillow back, 2 yards of white cording, a 12-inch-long white zipper, and a 13-inch pillow filler. For the pillow front you will need an 11-inch-square piece of orange print fabric, a 10½-inch-square piece of white cotton fabric, and scraps of beige calico fabric.

The additional materials required are: embroidery hoop, sewing needle, and orange sewing thread.

The appliquéd portion of the pillow may be done on a sewing machine with an appliqué stitch, or by hand.

Small amount of quilt batting to stuff the back of the finished chicken.

Dressmaker's carbon paper, tracing paper, and pencil.

Cutting the pieces

1. Patterns for each of the chicken appliqué pieces are given in **Figure A.** Enlarge them to full size and transfer them to the fabric colors as indicated.

2. Cut out each of the appliqué pieces, adding a ⅜-inch seam allowance around the edges.

3. Staystitch each of the pieces just barely outside the original pattern lines.

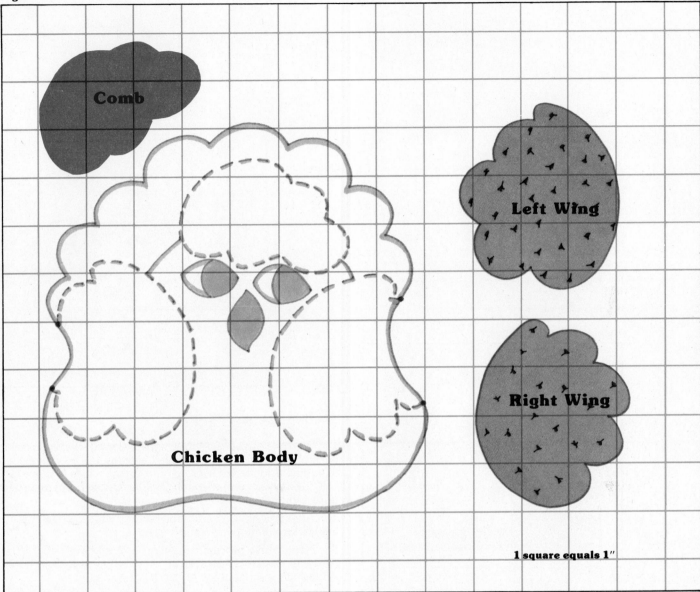

1 square equals 1"

Figure B

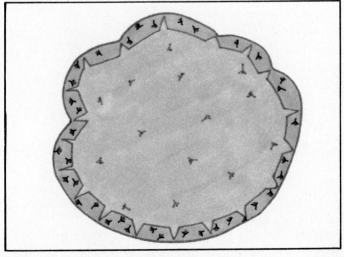

4. Press the seam allowance on each of the pattern pieces to the wrong side, clipping curves as you work so that the front of the piece is smooth and the edges are rounded **(Figure B).** The staystitching should not be visible on the right side.

Sewing the appliqués

1. Center and pin the chicken body on the right side of the 10½-inch-square orange fabric. Machine or hand appliqué the pattern in place, leaving it unstitched between small circles. The wings will later cover this section.

2. Pin the wings and comb appliqué pieces in place on top of the chicken body appliqué. Machine or hand stitch around each of the pieces.

3. Machine stitch the eyes, beak, and the lines between the comb and wings.

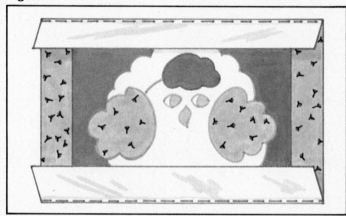

Figure D

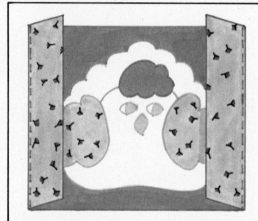

Figure C

Adding the padding

1. With the appliquéd fabric square wrong side up, slit the back of the fabric square behind the wings. Poke small pieces of batting through the slit to plump up the wings **(Figure C).** Only a small amount of batting will be required, but take care to distribute it evenly.

2. After you have inserted the batting, whipstitch the opening back together.

3. Repeat the process of slitting and stuffing behind the comb appliqué, the tail section, and the lower chicken body. Whipstitch the openings together.

4. Cut 2 pieces of beige calico fabric, each 2½ x 10½ inches. These will be the side panels for the finished pillow front.

5. Cut 2 pieces of white cotton fabric, each 2½ x 14 inches. They will be the top and bottom panels.

6. With right sides together, sew the 2 beige calico side panels to the appliquéd and padded square **(Figure D).** Sew a ½-inch seam, and press the seam toward the center panel.

7. Pin and sew the top and bottom white cotton panels to the center appliquéd square **(Figure E).** Press the seam toward the center square.

8. If you plan to use a purchased pillow, fold and press the sides of the completed pillow front to the wrong side of the front, matching the width and height of the pillow. Whipstitch the pressed pillow front to the purchased pillow using tiny invisible stitches.

9. Directions for sewing a pillow cover and adding the cording are included in the "Easy Applique Pillows" on page 120 of this book.

Baby Birth Keepsake

A three-dimensional fabric birth record that you personalize with baby's name and birthdate. Use your odds and ends of fabric, rick-rack, ribbon and trim to create a keepsake wall decoration.

Materials

18 x 24-inch piece of white or off-white linen-like fabric for the background.
Scraps of fabric for the appliqué pieces and sewing thread to match each color. Colors used for the appliqués are shown in **Figure A,** but feel free to change any of the colors that you wish.
Small amount of polyester batting to puff out the appliqués.
1 yard of narrow pink rick-rack.
1 foot of ¼-inch-wide pink satin ribbon.
1 yard of ¼-inch-wide blue satin ribbon.
1 skein each of green, white, and blue embroidery thread.
Embroidery hoop, embroidery needle, straight pins and scissors.
Dressmaker's carbon paper, tracing paper, and pencil.

Cutting and sewing the appliqués

1. Patterns for the appliquéd pieces are given in **Figure A.** Trace the pieces and use dressmaker's carbon paper to transfer them to the appropriate color of fabric. Cut out each of the

pieces, leaving a ½-inch-wide seam allowance around each piece.

2. Pin the appliqué pieces in place, arranging them in the center of the background fabric.

3. Full-size letters and numbers are provided for the child's name and birthdate in **Figure B.** Trace the appropriate letters onto a separate piece of paper.

4. Pin the blue satin border ribbon to the background fabric. Ease the ribbon on curves. It should be cut and turned under where it meets the appliqué positions. Whipstitch the ribbon in place, sewing with tiny invisible stitches on both edges.

5. Fold the fabric appliqué pieces on the pattern lines and iron the fold flat. Clip curves and corners where necessary.

6. Pin the appliqué pieces in place, and whipstitch around the outer edges, leaving a small space unstitched to insert the batting. Poke batting underneath the appliqué until the piece fills out slightly, then finish stitching.

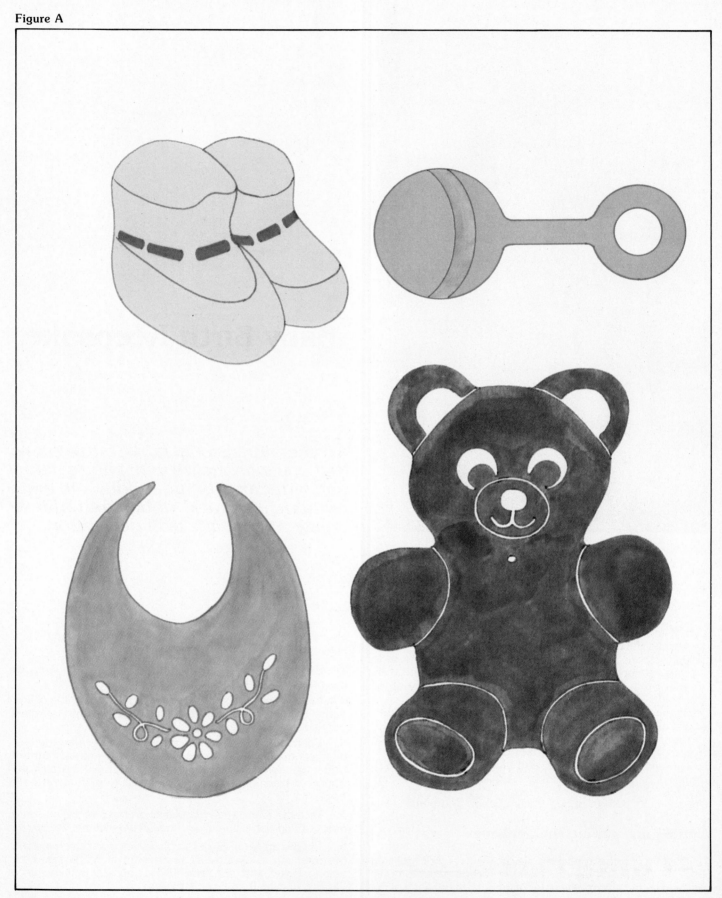

Finishing

1. Add the embroidered trim on the appliquéd pieces. The chain stitch is used for outlining and the satin stitch is worked on all solid areas: bear's features, bib flowers, bootie ties, alphabet letters and the stripe on the rattle.

2. Add the pink bow at the bear's neck, rick-rack around the bib, and the blue bow at the top.

3. Gently press the finished work with a steam iron and frame as you would any other picture.

Figure A

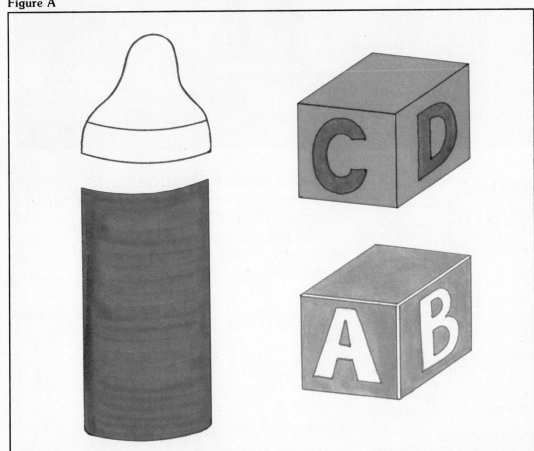

Figure B

ABCDEFGHIJKLMNOPQRST
UVWXYZabcdefghijklmnopqr
stuvwxyz01234 5 6789

Americana Weathervane

The traditional weathervane gets an updated and homey look by adding a plump fabric cover. It's a unique and beautiful piece of American heritage that will bring warmth and vitality to any room.

Materials

½ yard of calico fabric for the outer covering. Any small print or solid may be used. Large designs are not suitable for this project.

Needle and sewing thread to match the fabric.

Any one of several different materials may be used for the inner support on the horse. It may be cut from ½-inch-thick plywood using a coping saw, or from a sheet of ½-inch-thick styrofoam using a razor knife. You will need 1 piece 9 x 17 inches.

A ¼-inch-diameter wooden dowel rod 10 inches long.

A slice of natural log for the base of the stand. Any other heavy material may be substituted.

Hand drill and ¼-inch drill bit to drill a hole in the base and into the bottom of the inner support.

White glue, scissors, fine sandpaper (if you use plywood for the inner support), and a steam iron.

A 17 x 18-inch piece of thin (3-ply) quilt batting.

Straight pins or push pins.

Dressmaker's carbon paper, tracing paper, and pencil.

Cutting the inner support

1. Enlarge the horse pattern given in **Figure A** to full size, and transfer it to the plywood or styrofoam.

2. Cut out the inner support, carefully following the pattern lines. If you have used plywood, smooth the edges on the inner support with sandpaper to eliminate any splinters.

3. Drill a hole ¼ inch in diameter into the bottom edge of the inner support to accommodate the wood dowel rod. The position for this hole is indicated on the pattern (Figure A).

Cutting and sewing the fabric

1. Use the same enlarged pattern to trace a fabric front and back for the horse onto the wrong side of the fabric, adding a ⅜-inch seam allowance around the outer edges.

2. Cut and hem together 1½-inch-wide strips of fabric until you have one continuous border strip, 72 inches long. This strip will be used to cover the inner support.

3. Beginning at the bottom where the stand will be inserted, pin the border strip to the horse front, sewing a ⅜-inch-wide seam all the way around the horse **(Figure B).** Ease the strip on corners and curves. Work slowly and carefully to make sure that you are following the traced horse pattern exactly. Extra effort at this point will result in a professional-looking finished project.

152

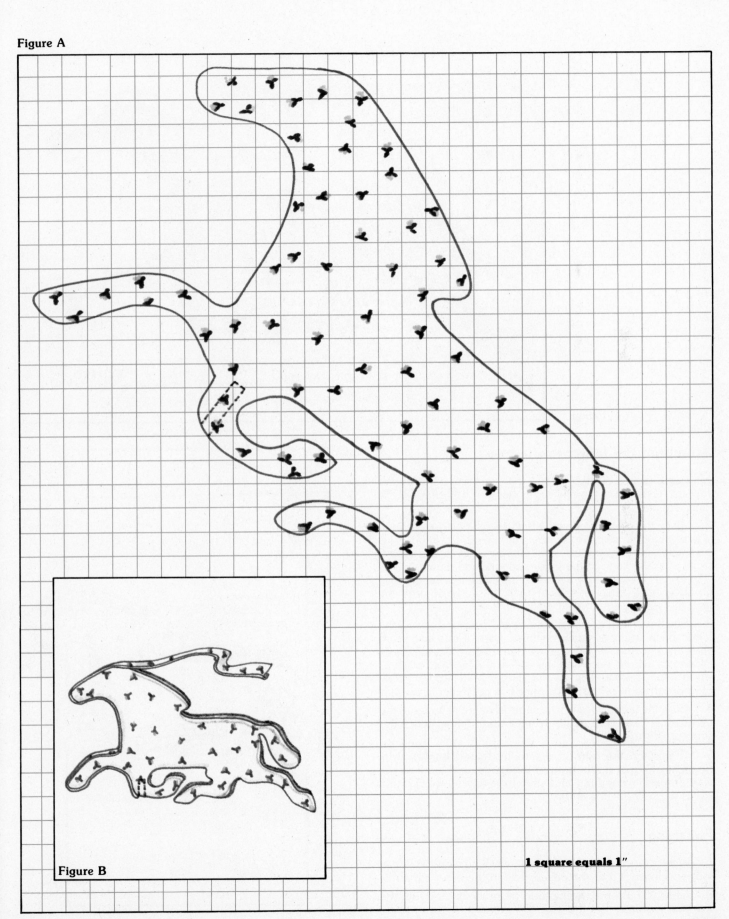

Figure B

1 square equals 1"

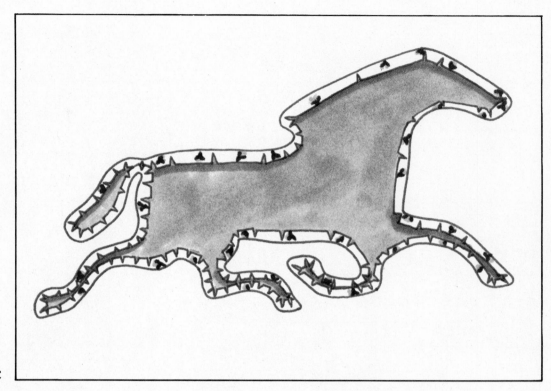

Figure C

Attaching the fabric to the base

1. Cut 2 pieces of quilt batting the same size as the inner support. Glue the batting pieces in place on both sides of the inner support.

2. Place the fabric front with attached fabric strip over one side of the inner support. Gently pull the fabric so that it fits smoothly over the support. Fold the raw edges of the border strips over the back of the inner support, and glue in place. Clip excess fabric where necessary so that it lies flat (**Figure C**). Use push pins or straight pins to secure it until the glue dries.

3. Stitch just barely outside the traced pattern lines on the fabric back using a small machine stitch. Press the seam allowance to the wrong side of the fabric. Clip the seam allowance where necessary to make the pressed edge as smooth as possible. The staystitching should not be visible on the right side of the fabric after it is pressed.

4. Glue the fabric back on the support over the edges of the fabric strip. It should be flush with the edge of the inner support (**Figure D**).

5. Whipstitch the fabric back to the glued border strip. Begin stitching at the bottom of the horse, and work all the way around, smoothing and stretching as you go. Do not cover the hole for the stand.

Finishing

1. Wipe glue on the end of the 10-inch-long wooden dowel rod, and insert it into the drilled hole in the inner support.

2. Glue and insert the other end of the dowel rod into the wooden log base. Let the glue dry overnight.

Figure D

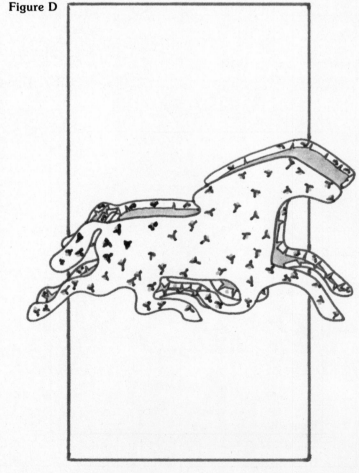

Happy Birthday Pillow

A beautiful and very personal way to remember that special someone. Or change the message to record any happy event.

Materials

16-inch-square piece of white cotton eyelet fabric (or any other fabric suitable for embroidery) for the pillow front. To line the eyelet you can use a 16-inch-square piece of plain white cotton or a contrasting color which will show through the eyelet. Sew the eyelet and the lining pieces together on all 4 outer edges before beginning work.

Scraps of embroidery thread for the flowers. A suggested color chart is provided in **Figure A,** but you can change any of the colors you wish. This is a great project to use up all of your leftover embroidery thread.

Embroidery hoop, embroidery needle, scissors, ironing board, straight pins, and steam iron.

14-inch-square polyester pillow filler.

12-inch zipper ("invisible" or in a color that matches the fabric you chose for the backing).

For the back of the pillow, you will need a 17 x 16-inch piece of fabric. You can use the eyelet fabric again, or pick up any color from the flower design.

2 yards of white eyelet ruffle, approximately 2 inches wide.

Sewing thread to match the backing fabric.

Dressmaker's carbon paper, tracing paper, and pencil.

Working the design

1. The pattern for the center of the pillow is provided full size in **Figure A.** Use dressmaker's carbon paper to transfer the design to the center of the 16-inch eyelet pillow front. You can enlarge our "Happy Birthday" lettering, but it is more personal if you letter it yourself. Draw it first on a piece of paper; then transfer it to the fabric using dressmaker's carbon paper.

2. Place the eyelet pillow front in an embroidery hoop and embroider each of the flowers. Use the satin stitch for all small solid areas such as small leaves, petals and flower centers. Use the split stitch for all narrow lines such as the stems on the leaves and for outlining the "Happy Birthday" message. Use French knots on all small circles such as the very tiny flowers. The long-and-short stitch is used for areas which are large and solid such as on the lavender iris and the red tulip.

3. When the work is completed, press the needlework gently on the wrong side.

1 square equals 1″

Happy Birthday

Sewing the pillow

1. Fold the 17 x 16-inch fabric rectangle along the 17-inch side and cut along the fold to form 2 pieces 8½ x 16 inches **(Figure B)**.

2. Install the zipper (as directed on the package) between the two 16-inch edges, and press the seams open.

3. Place the finished needlework right side up on a flat surface.

4. Pin the eyelet ruffle trim around the outside of the 14-inch embroidered pillow front, with the ruffle facing in toward the center and the bound edge facing out. Allow a very generous amount of trim at all 4 corners of the pillow. When the pillow is turned right side out the trim will require enough fullness to turn the corner. Begin and end the trim at the bottom center of the pillow.

5. Stitch along the edge of the trim, through all the layers including the pillow front. To eliminate floppy corners on the finished work, gradually taper the sides in toward the corners so the middle of each side is about ½ inch fuller than the corners, thus making all four sides bow out slightly **(Figure C)**.

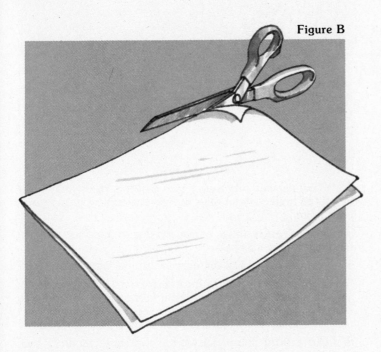

Figure B

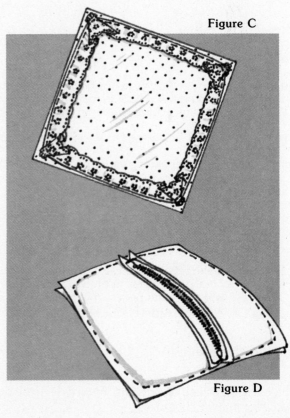

Figure C

6. Place the fabric back (right side down and with the zipper open) on top of the needlework front. Trim will be between the front and back. Pin the front and back together. Stitch around the outside edges, through the fabric back, trim, and needlework front **(Figure D)**.

7. Trim all the edges to ⅜ inch and clip the corners.

8. Turn the pillow right side out and press it with a steam iron. Insert the pillow filler and zip up the back.

Figure D

Padded Fabric Frames

Making these picture frames is a little like eating peanuts – once you start, you can't stop! They're great sellers at a bazaar, and you'll want to make extras for yourself. It's a very special gift for Grandma with a picture of her grand-child tucked inside.

Materials

Double-thickness mounting board (available from art or draft-
ing stores). The small square frame requires a piece 8 x
20 inches; the larger curved frame requires a piece 5 x 26
inches.
½ yard of fabric will be enough to make either size frame.
1 yard of lace trim.
A piece of bonded quilt batting the same size as the finished
frame.
White glue.
Needle and sewing thread.
Straight pins, scissors, metal ruler, pencil and a razor knife.
Iron and ironing board.
Fine sandpaper, toothpicks, and clothespins (or spring-type
clamps).
If you plan to make several of these frames, we suggest that
you invest in a can of spray adhesive. It is rather expen-
sive, but will make the project much faster and easier.
Spray adhesive can usually be found at art supply stores.

Cutting the pieces

1. Use a ruler and pencil to carefully mark and transfer the front, back, and stand dimensions (**Figure A**) to the double-thickness mounting board.

2. Carefully cut out each piece using a razor knife. It is helpful to hold a metal ruler against the cutting line to guide your knife.

3. Smooth any uneven or frayed edges of the boards with a piece of fine sandpaper.

4. Use the boards as patterns to cut the fabric coverings.

5. Trace the outline of the front board onto the wrong side of a piece of fabric. Cut out the front fabric covering, adding a 2-inch-wide border on all 4 outer edges. The border will provide enough extra fabric to overlap the edges of the frame.

6. Cut a front lining piece from the same fabric, 1 inch smaller on all 4 edges than the front board. Mark the center window.

7. Center and pin the front lining over the front covering, right sides together (**Figure B**).

8. Double stitch around the center window using a very small machine stitch.

9. Cut out the center window, ¼ inch from the stitching line. Clip corners as close to the stitching line as possible without cutting the stitching itself (**Figure C**).

Figure A

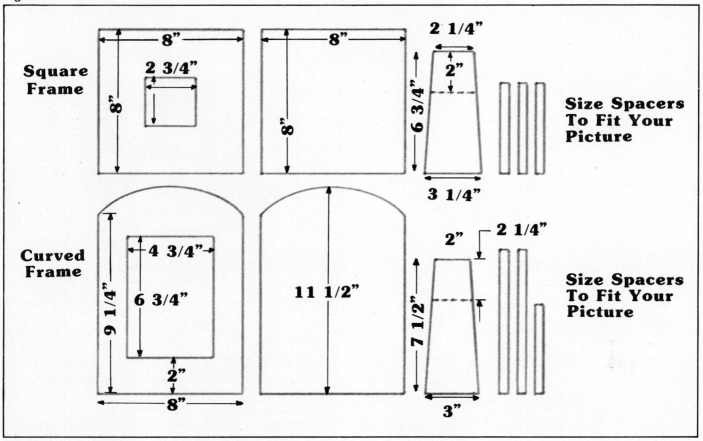

Square Frame

8"
8"
2 3/4"

8"
8"

2 1/4"
2"
6 3/4"
3 1/4"

Size Spacers To Fit Your Picture

Curved Frame

9 1/4"
4 3/4"
6 3/4"
2"
8"

11 1/2"

2"
2 1/4"
7 1/2"
3"

Size Spacers To Fit Your Picture

Figure B

Figure C

Figure D

Figure E

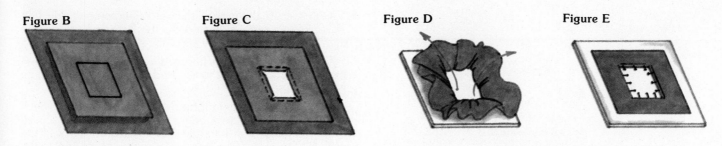

Figure F

10. Turn the assembled front right side out and press carefully.

11. Cut a piece of quilt batting the same size as the front board, cutting out the center window. Glue the batting to the front board.

12. Pull the fabric front covering through the center window of the front board, leaving the smaller front lining still on the unquilted back **(Figure D).**

13. Wipe or spray glue on the unquilted side of the front board. Stretch and pull the front lining until it fits flat on the mounting board and the window seam is straight and even. If you use white glue, stick straight pins around the window seams to hold the fabric in place until the glue dries **(Figure E).**

14. Wipe or spray glue on the outer edges of the wrong side of the front fabric covering. Stretch and smooth the fabric over the batting and secure it to the frame (over the lining fabric). Clip corners to eliminate fabric bulk **(Figure F).**

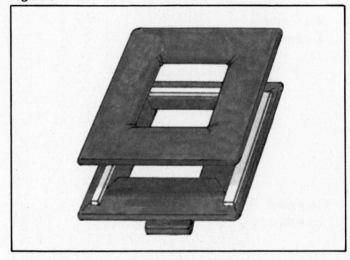

Figure J

Making the stand

1. Trace the stand onto the wrong side of a double thickness of fabric. Cut out, adding a ½-inch-wide seam allowance on all sides.

2. Place the resulting stand-covering pieces right sides together and sew a ⅜-inch seam around the edges, leaving the bottom edge open and unstitched **(Figure G).** Turn the fabric cover right side out.

3. Lightly score the mounting board stand on one side with a razor knife where indicated by the broken lines on the pattern in Figure A. This will allow the stand to bend evenly.

4. Slip the stand board inside the stand cover. Turn the bottom raw edges to the inside and whipstitch the opening together **(Figure H).**

5. Position the completed stand on the fabric-covered back of the frame, with the lower edges even **(Figure I).** The scored side of the stand board should face toward the back of the frame. Glue the top of the stand (above the scored line) to the frame. Clamp tightly and let the glue dry overnight.

Finishing

1. Cut 3 spacers from the mounting board, following the dimensions given in Figure A.

2. Glue and clamp the covered front and back frame pieces together, sandwiching the spacer boards between them on the top and sides **(Figure J).** Do not use spray adhesive for this step; only white glue. Clamp the frame overnight using either clothespins or spring clamps.

3. Use a toothpick to carefully spread glue between the front and back of the assembled frame. Carefully insert lace trim between the glued edges. Begin at the bottom of one side, and work up to the top, across, and back down the opposite side. Allow a generous amount of lace at the 2 top corners in order to turn the corners without pulling. Let the glue dry overnight.

4. Mount your picture on a piece of board slightly larger than the window opening. Insert the picture into the slot at the bottom of completed frame.

Figure G

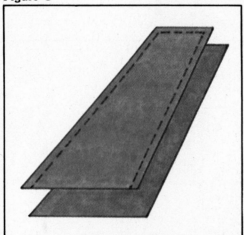

Figure H

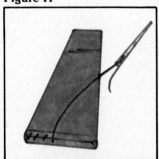

Figure I

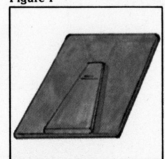

15. Trace the back board onto the wrong side of a piece of fabric. Cut out, adding a 2-inch-wide border on all sides.

16. Cover the back board with the back covering, stretching it until it is smooth, and overlapping and gluing the edges on the opposite side of the board.

160